play guitar with...

D1079061

Franz
Ferdinand

Wise Publications
part of The Music Sales Group
London/New York/Paris/Sydney/Copenhagen/Berlin/Madrid/Tokyo

Published by
Wise Publications
8/9 Frith Street,
London W1D 3JB, England

Exclusive Distributors:
Music Sales Limited
Distribution Centre, Newmarket Road,
Bury St Edmunds, Suffolk IP33 3YB
Music Sales Pty Limited
120 Rothschild Avenue,
Rosebery, NSW 2018, Australia

Order No. AM91768
ISBN 0-7119-3889-X
This book © Copyright 2005
by Wise Publications

Music arranged by Arthur Dick
Music processed by Paul Ewers Music Design
Cover designed by Fresh Lemon
Printed in Malta

CD recorded, mixed and mastered by
John Rose & Jonas Persson
Guitars by Arthur Dick
Bass by Paul Townsend
Drums by Brett Morgan

Your Guarantee of Quality

As publishers, we strive to produce
every book to the highest commercial standards.
The music has been freshly engraved and the book has
been carefully designed to minimise awkward page turns
and to make playing from it a real pleasure.
Particular care has been given to specifying acid-free,
neutral-sized paper made from pulps which have not been
elemental chlorine bleached. This pulp is from farmed
sustainable forests and was produced with
special regard for the environment.
Throughout, the printing and binding have been planned
to ensure a sturdy, attractive publication which
should give years of enjoyment.
If your copy fails to meet our high standards,
please inform us and we will gladly replace it.

www.musicsales.com

guitar tablature explained

Guitar music can be notated in three different ways: on a musical stave, in tablature, and in rhythm slashes.

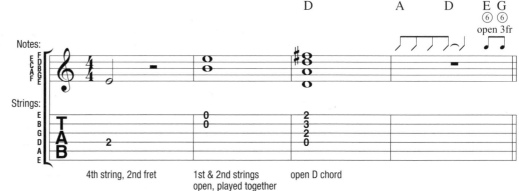

RHYTHM SLASHES are written above the stave. Strum chords in the rhythm indicated. Round noteheads indicate single notes.

THE MUSICAL STAVE shows pitches and rhythms and is divided by lines into bars. Pitches are named after the first seven letters of the alphabet.

TABLATURE graphically represents the guitar fingerboard. Each horizontal line represents a string, and each number represents a fret.

4th string, 2nd fret

1st & 2nd strings open, played together

open D chord

definitions for special guitar notation

SEMI-TONE BEND: Strike the note and bend up a semi-tone (1/2 step).

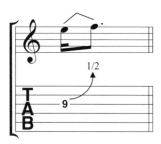

WHOLE-TONE BEND: Strike the note and bend up a whole-tone (whole step).

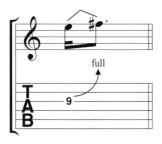

GRACE NOTE BEND: Strike the note and bend as indicated. Play the first note as quickly as possible.

QUARTER-TONE BEND: Strike the note and bend up a 1/4 step.

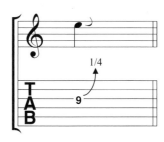

BEND & RELEASE: Strike the note and bend up as indicated, then release back to the original note.

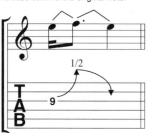

COMPOUND BEND & RELEASE: Strike the note and bend up and down in the rhythm indicated.

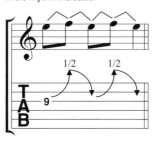

PRE-BEND: Bend the note as indicated, then strike it.

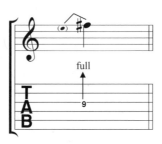

PRE-BEND & RELEASE: Bend the note as indicated. Strike it and release the note back to the original pitch.

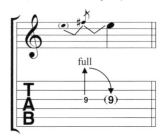

UNISON BEND: Strike the two notes simultaneously and bend the lower note up to the pitch of the higher.

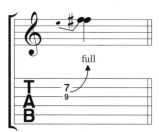

BEND & RESTRIKE: Strike the note and bend as indicated then restrike the string where the symbol occurs.

BEND, HOLD AND RELEASE: Same as bend and release but hold the bend for the duration of the tie.

BEND AND TAP: Bend the note as indicated and tap the higher fret while still holding the bend.

VIBRATO: The string is vibrated by rapidly bending and releasing the note with the fretting hand.

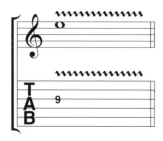

HAMMER-ON: Strike the first note with one finger, then sound the second note (on the same string) with another finger by fretting it without picking.

PULL-OFF: Place both fingers on the notes to be sounded, strike the first note and without picking, pull the finger off to sound the second note.

LEGATO SLIDE (GLISS): Strike the first note and then slide the same fret-hand finger up or down to the second note. The second note is not struck.

NOTE: The speed of any bend is indicated by the music notation and tempo.

4

SHIFT SLIDE (GLISS & RESTRIKE): Same as legato slide, except the second note is struck.

TRILL: Very rapidly alternate between the notes indicated by continuously hammering on and pulling off.

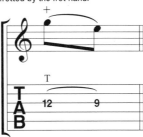

TAPPING: Hammer ("tap") the fret indicated with the pick-hand index or middle finger and pull off to the note fretted by the fret hand.

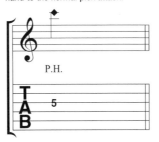

PICK SCRAPE: The edge of the pick is rubbed down (or up) the string, producing a scratchy sound.

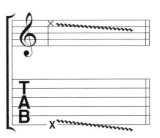

MUFFLED STRINGS: A percussive sound is produced by laying the fret hand across the string(s) without depressing, and striking them with the pick hand.

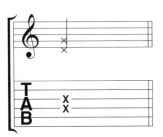

NATURAL HARMONIC: Strike the note while the fret-hand lightly touches the string directly over the fret indicated.

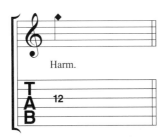

PINCH HARMONIC: The note is fretted normally and a harmonic is produced by adding the edge of the thumb or the tip of the index finger of the pick hand to the normal pick attack.

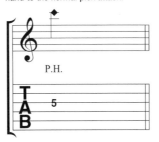

HARP HARMONIC: The note is fretted normally and a harmonic is produced by gently resting the pick hand's index finger directly above the indicated fret (in brackets) while plucking the appropriate string.

PALM MUTING: The note is partially muted by the pick hand lightly touching the string(s) just before the bridge.

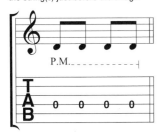

RAKE: Drag the pick across the strings indicated with a single motion.

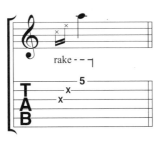

TREMOLO PICKING: The note is picked as rapidly and continuously as possible.

ARPEGGIATE: Play the notes of the chord indicated by quickly rolling them from bottom to top.

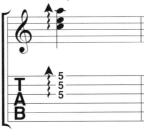

SWEEP PICKING: Rhythmic downstroke and/or upstroke motion across the strings.

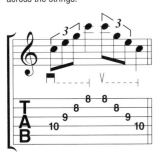

VIBRATO DIVE BAR AND RETURN: The pitch of the note or chord is dropped a specific number of steps (in rhythm) then returned to the original pitch.

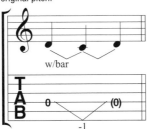

VIBRATO BAR SCOOP: Depress the bar just before striking the note, then quickly release the bar.

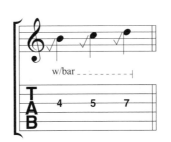

VIBRATO BAR DIP: Strike the note and then immediately drop a specific number of steps, then release back to the original pitch.

additional musical definitions

 (accent) • Accentuate note (play it louder).

 (accent) • Accentuate note with great intensity.

(staccato) • Shorten time value of note.

 • Downstroke

 • Upstroke

D.%. al Coda • Go back to the sign (%), then play until the bar marked *To Coda* ⊕ then skip to the section marked ⊕ *Coda*.

D.C. al Fine • Go back to the beginning of the song and play until the bar marked *Fine*.

tacet • Instrument is silent (drops out).

 • Repeat bars between signs.

1. **2.** • When a repeated section has different endings, play the first ending only the first time and the second ending only the second time.

NOTE: Tablature numbers in brackets mean:
1. The note is sustained, but a new articulation (such as hammer on or slide) begins.
2. A note may be fretted but not necessarily played.

jacqueline

Words & Music by Alexander Kapranos, Nicholas McCarthy & Robert Hardy

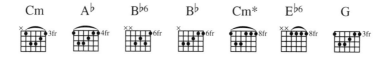

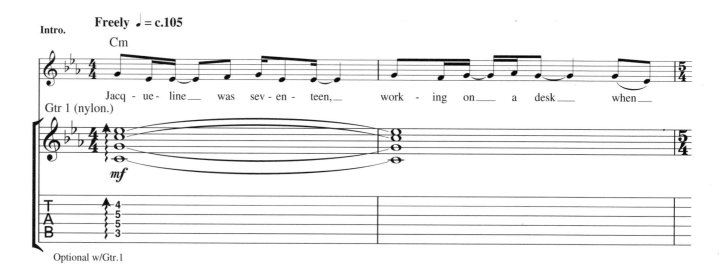

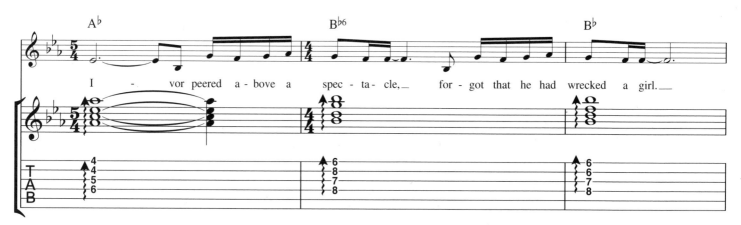

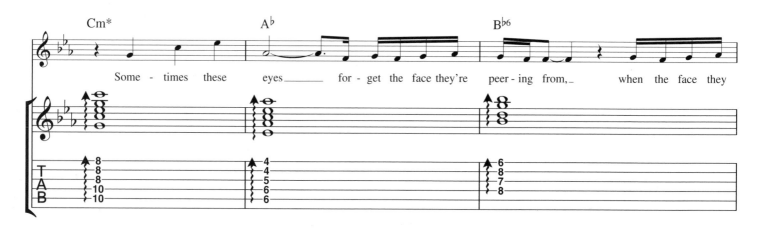

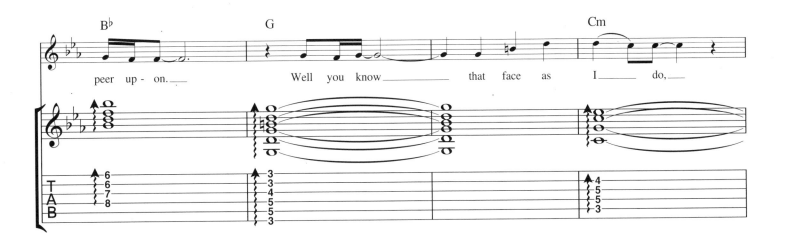

peer up - on.___ Well you know___ that face as I___ do,___

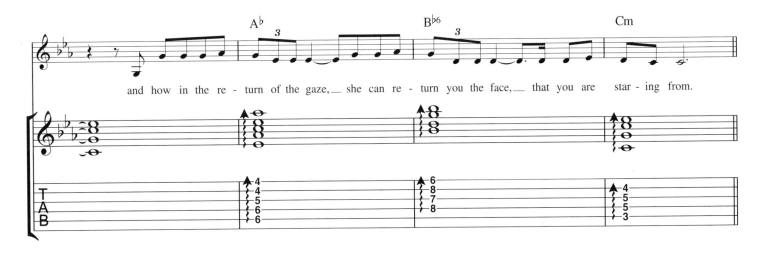

and how in the re - turn of the gaze,___ she can re - turn you the face,___ that you are star - ing from.

♩ = 152

Bass cued for gtr.

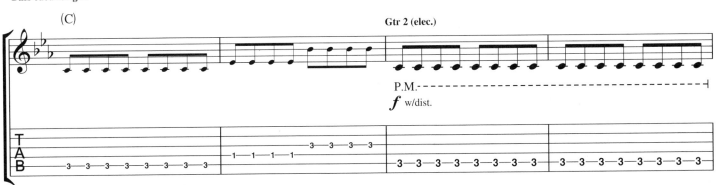

(C)

Gtr 2 (elec.)

P.M.----------------------

f w/dist.

Cm

* Gtr 3 (elec.) dbls.

*chords implied by harmony. Play Gtr.3 part

It's always better on holiday,_____ so much better on holiday.

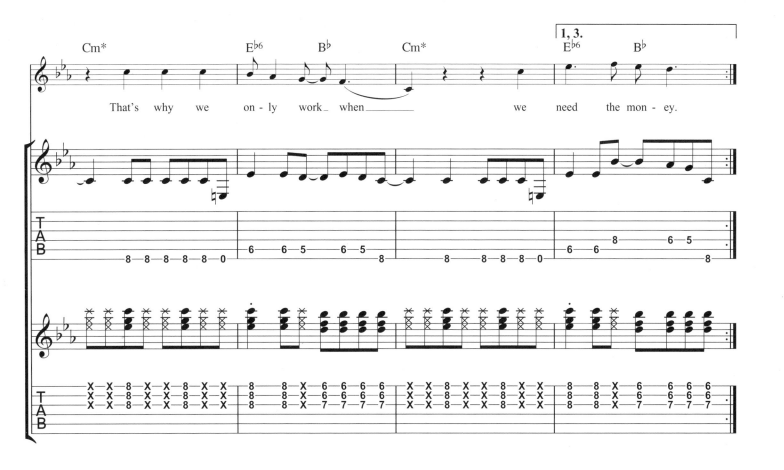

That's why we on - ly work_ when ___ we need the mon - ey.

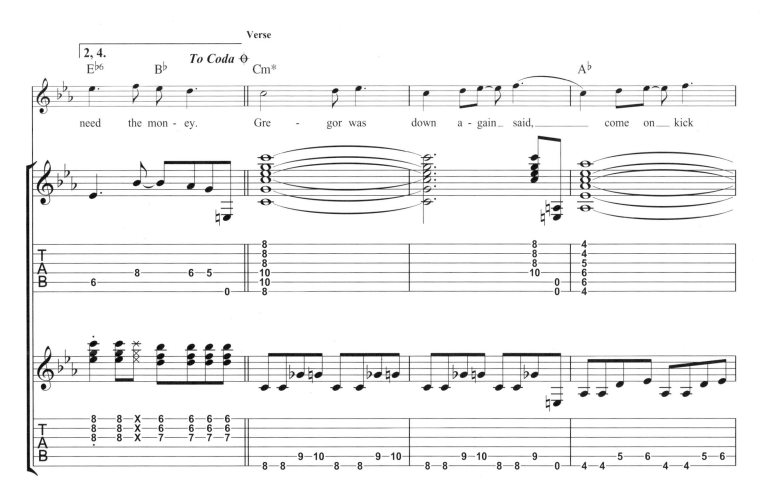

need the mon - ey. Gre - gor was down a - gain_ said, ___ come on_ kick

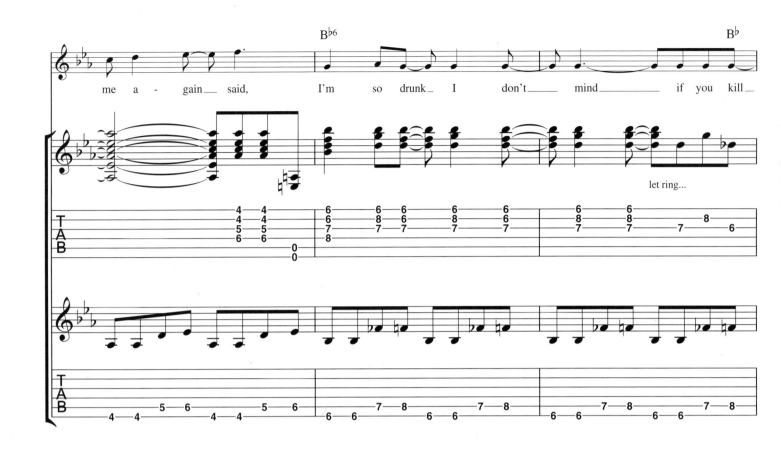

me a - gain___ said, I'm so drunk___ I don't___ mind___ if you kill

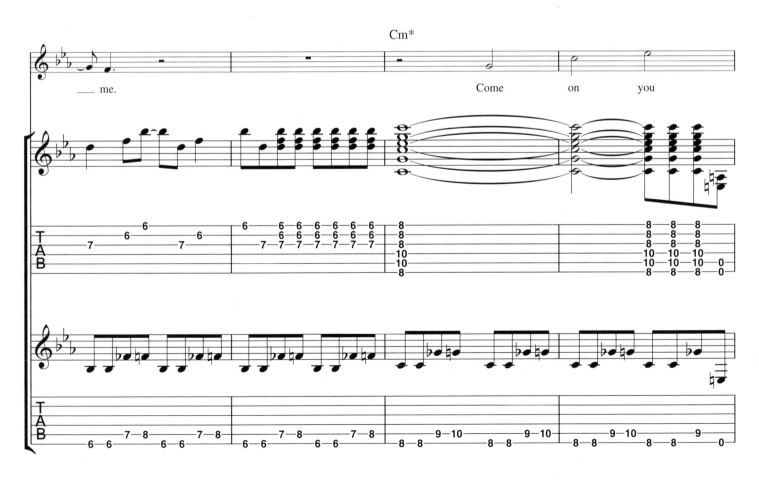

___ me. Come on you

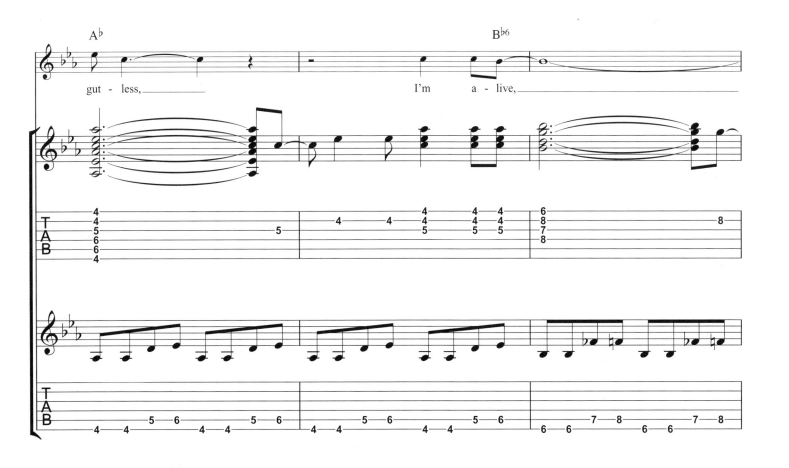

gut - less,_____ I'm a - live,_____

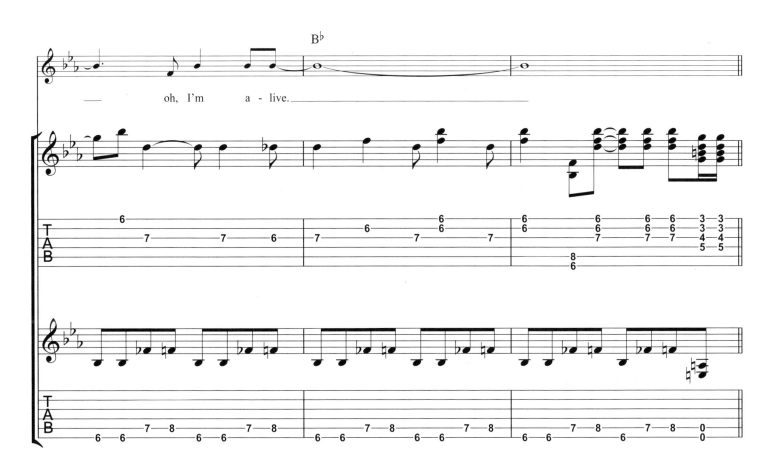

_____ oh, I'm a - live._____

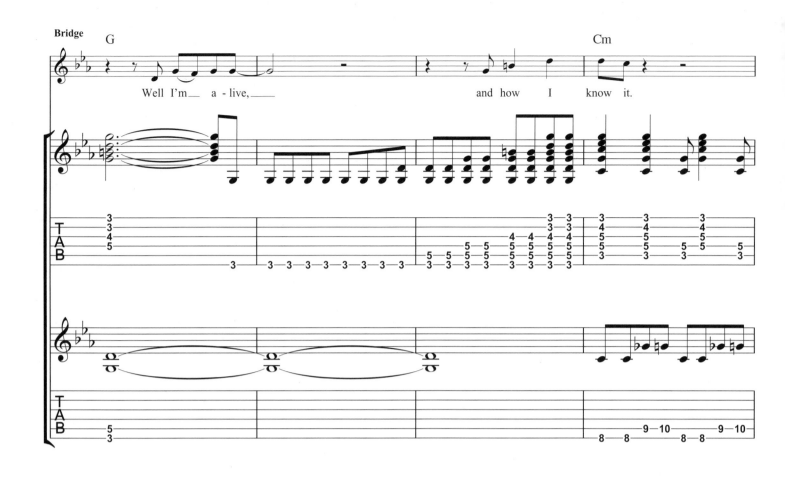

Well I'm a-live, and how I know it.

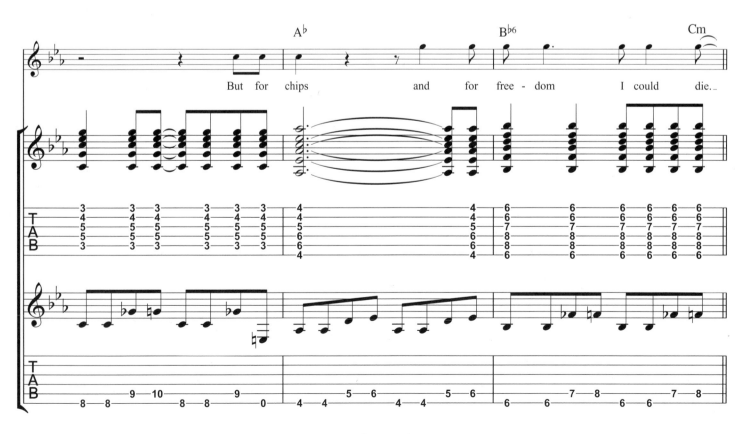

But for chips and for free-dom I could die.

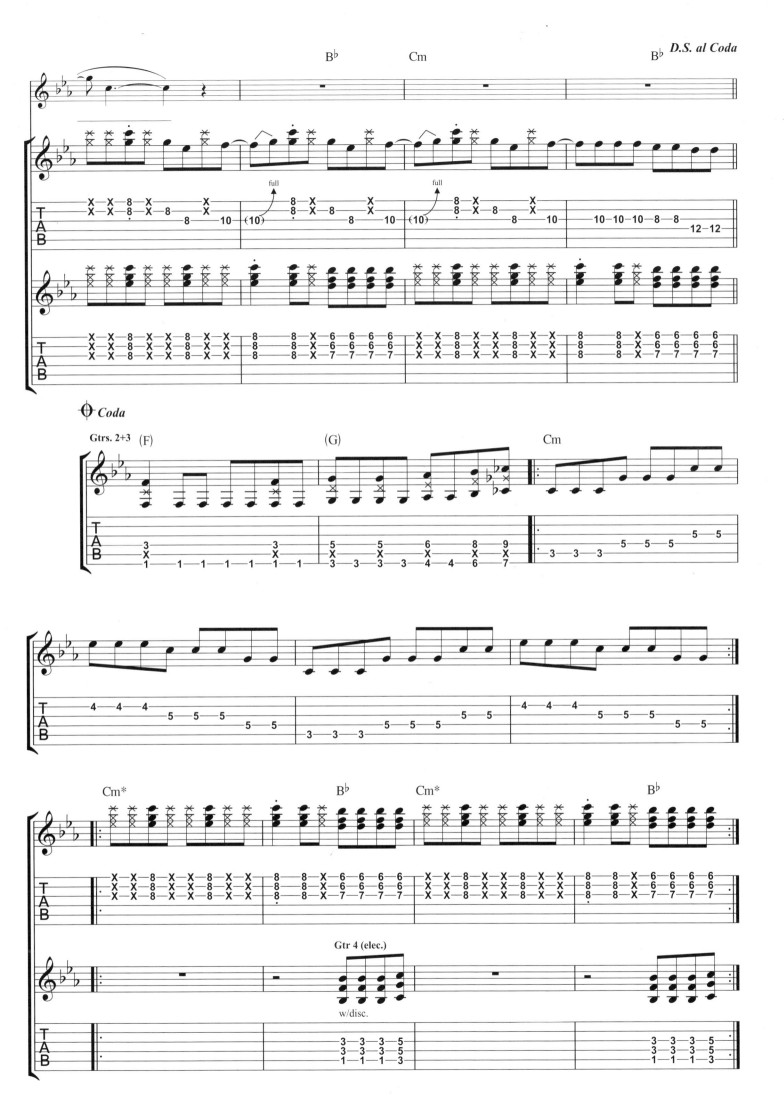

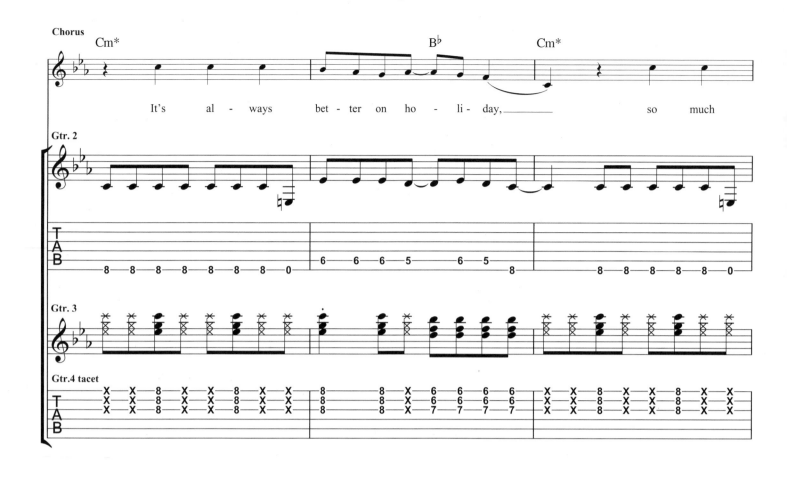

It's al - ways bet - ter on ho - li - day,_____ so much

bet - ter on ho - li - day. That's why we on - ly work__ when_____

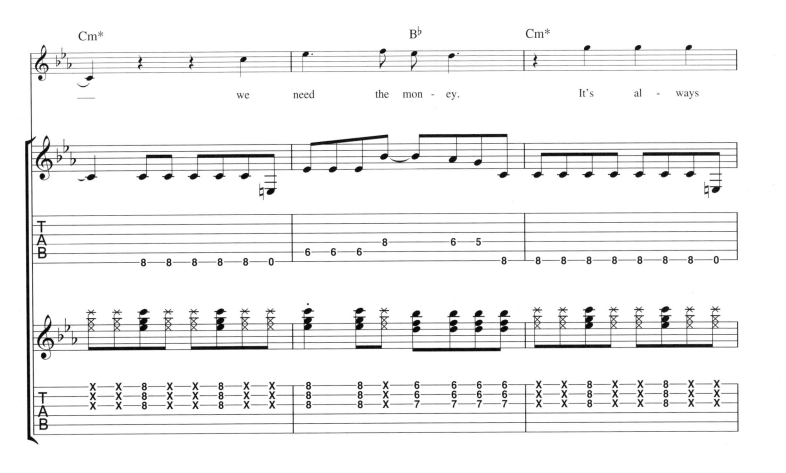

we need the mon - ey. It's al - ways

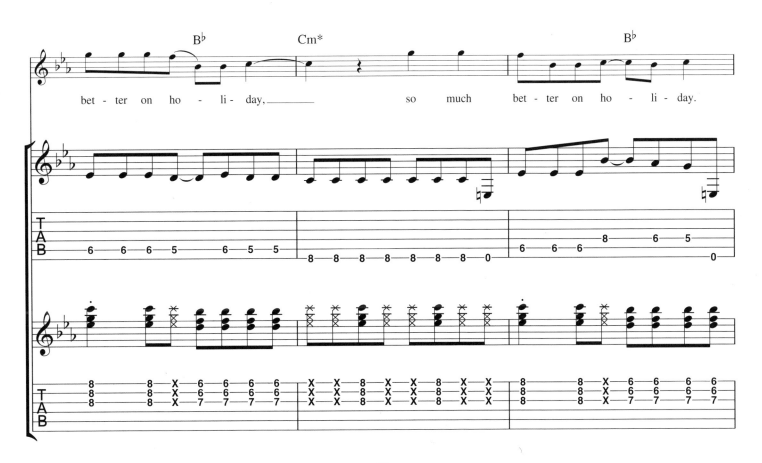

bet - ter on ho - li - day, _____ so much bet - ter on ho - li - day.

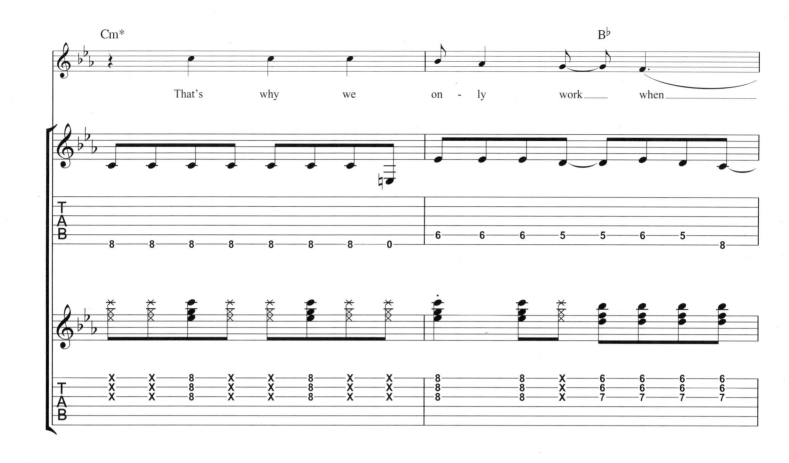

That's why we on - ly work when

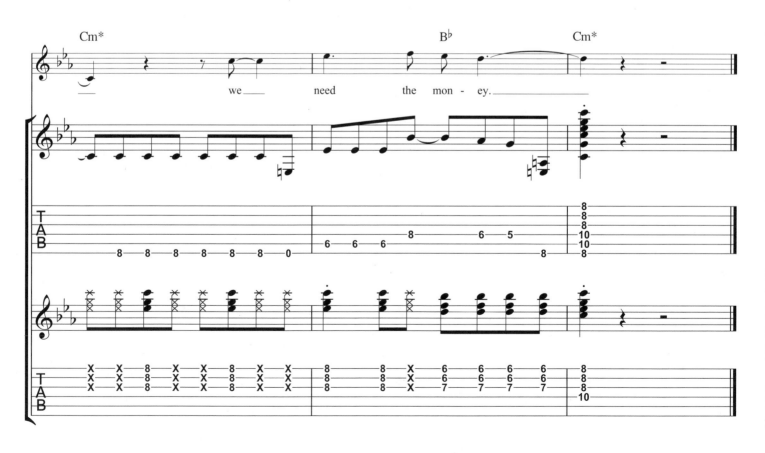

we need the mon - ey.

tell her tonight

Words & Music by Alexander Kapranos & Nicholas McCarthy

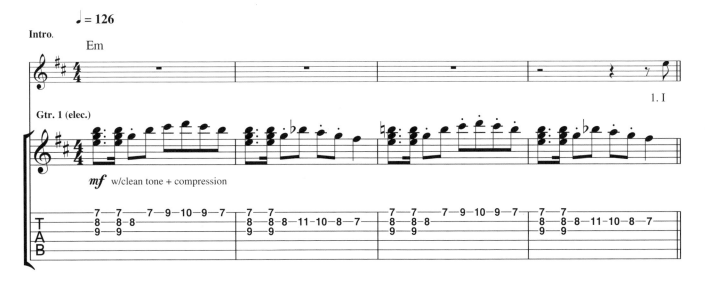

2 bars count in:

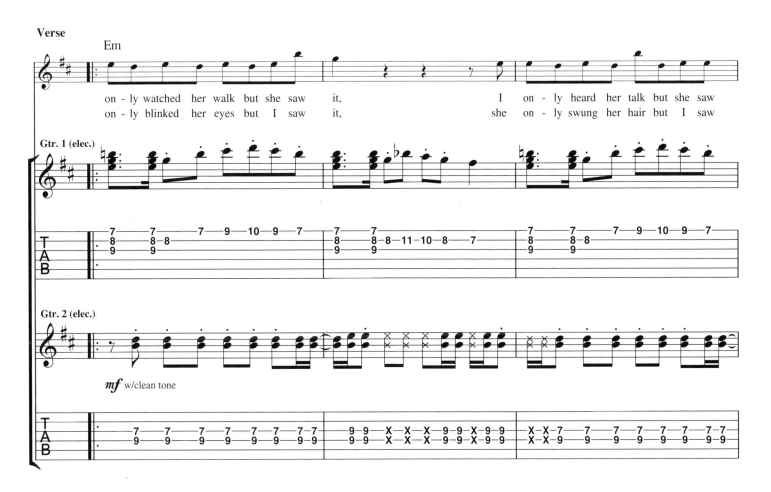

only watched her walk but she saw it,   I only heard her talk but she saw
only blinked her eyes but I saw it,   she only swung her hair but I saw

it.   I   on - ly touched her hips but she saw
it.   She   on - ly shook her hips but I saw

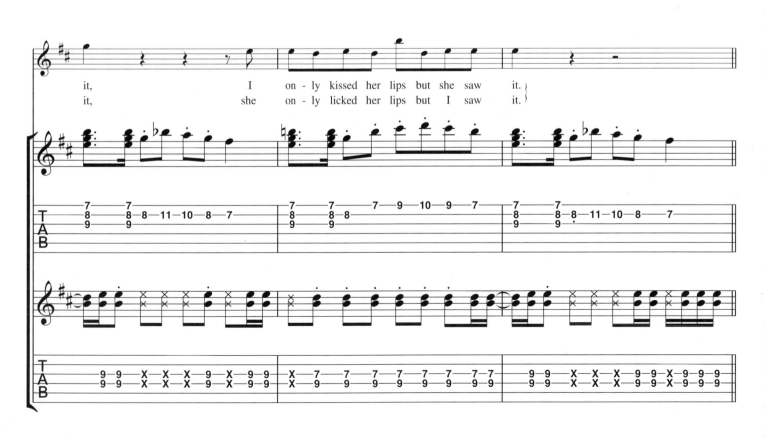

it,   I   on - ly kissed her lips but she saw   it.
it,   she   on - ly licked her lips but I saw   it.

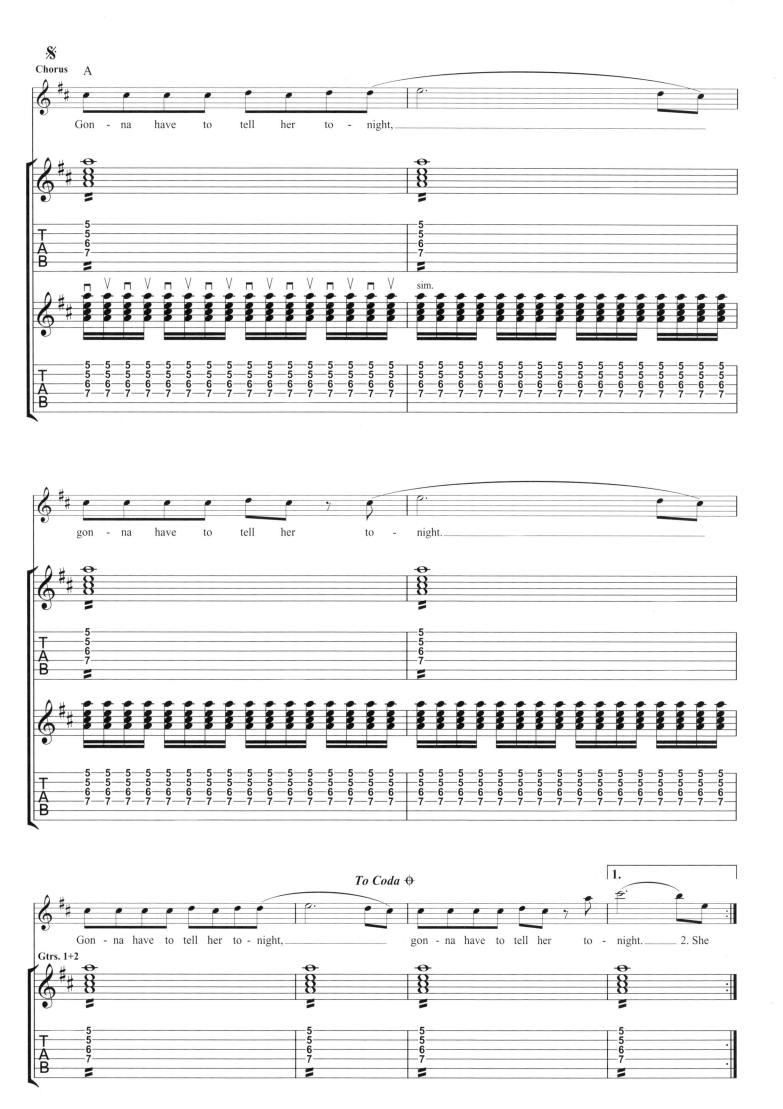

D.S. al Coda

Coda

Bridge

21

take me out

Words & Music by Alexander Kapranos & Nicholas McCarthy

2 bars count in:

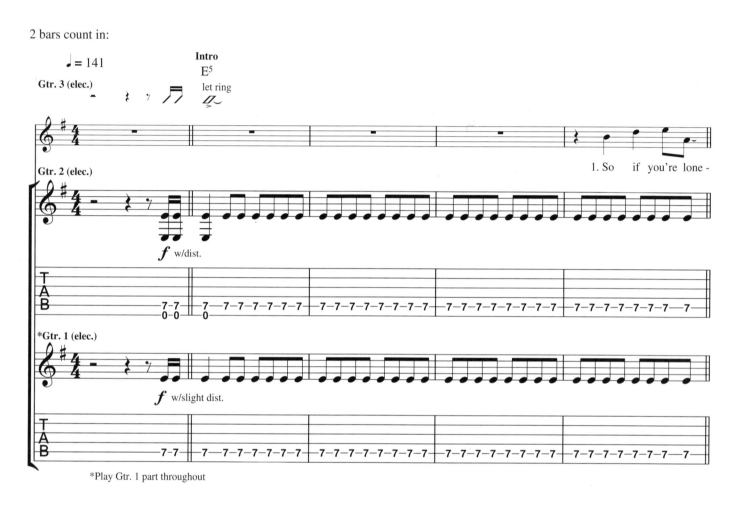

*Play Gtr. 1 part throughout

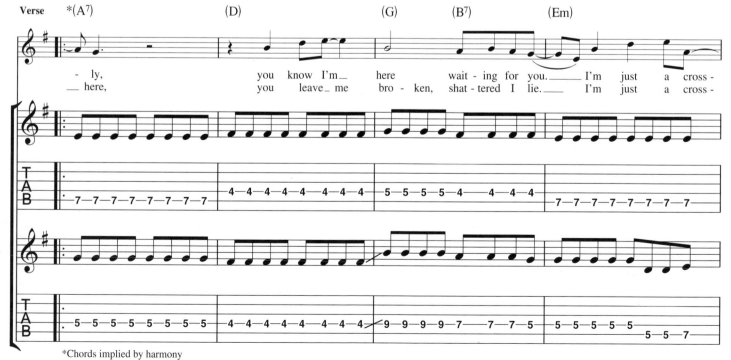

*Chords implied by harmony

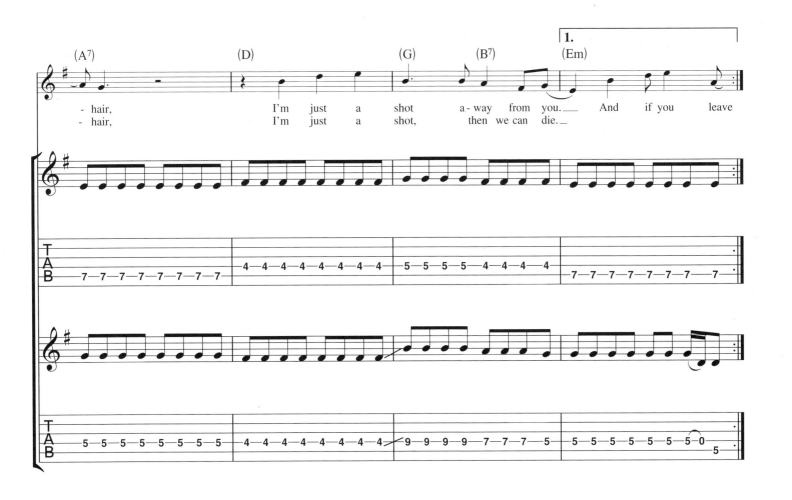

- hair,   I'm just a shot a-way from you.___ And if you leave
- hair,   I'm just a shot, then we can die.___

Aah,___

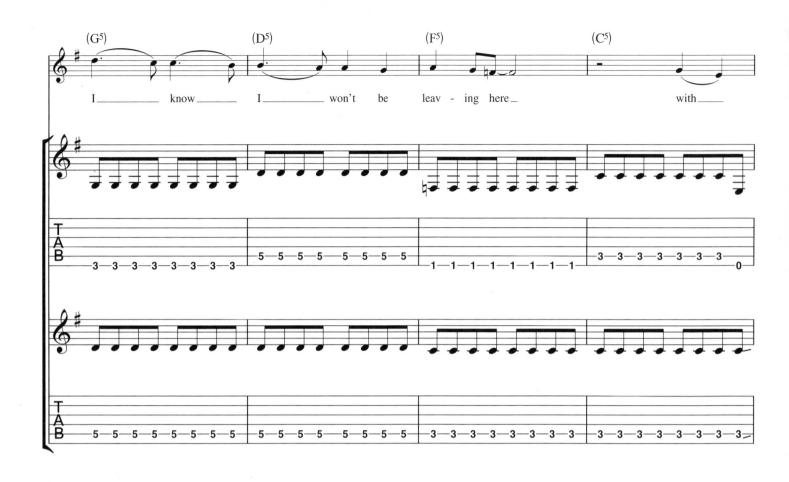

I _____ know _____ I _____ won't be leav - ing here _____ with _____

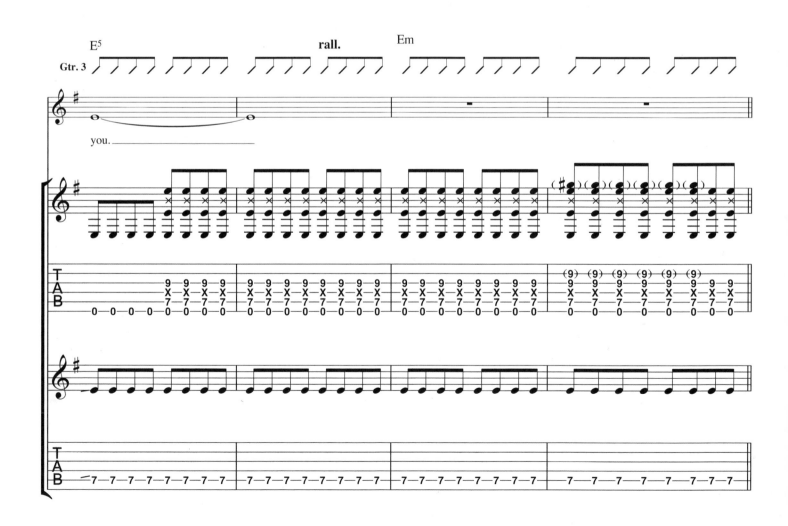

you. _____

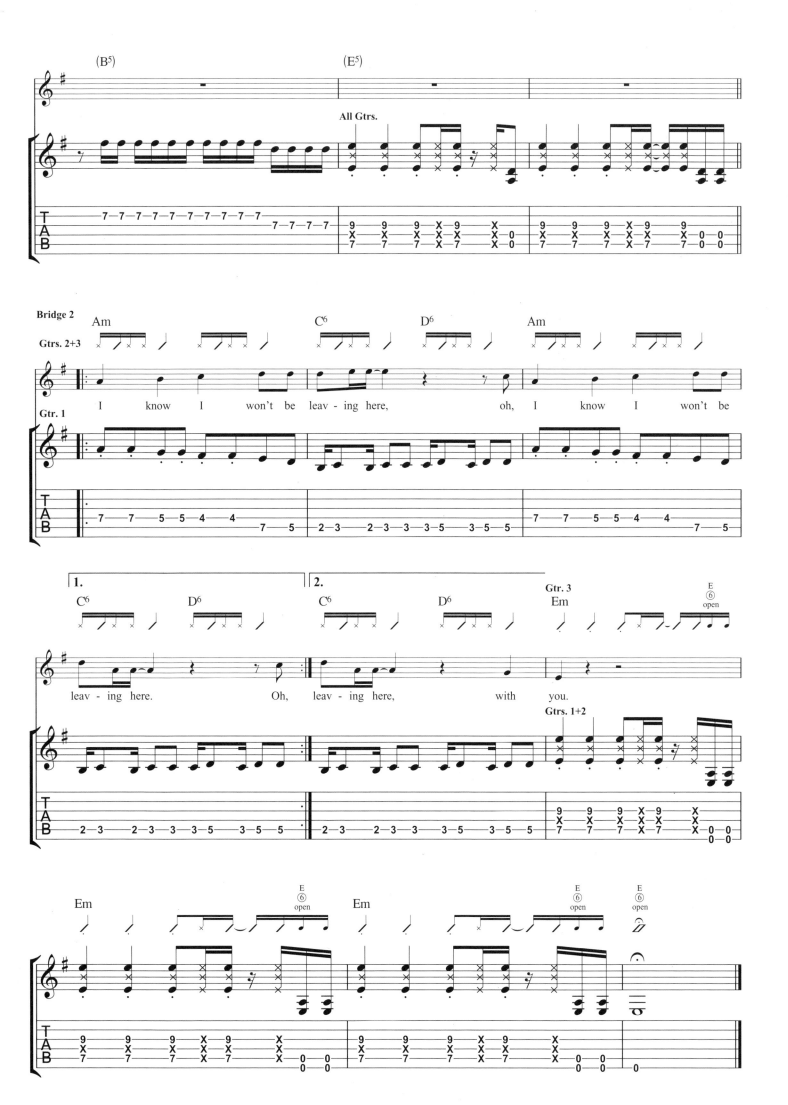

the dark of the matinée

Words & Music by Alexander Kapranos, Nicholas McCarthy & Robert Hardy

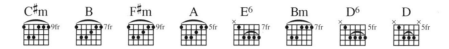

2 bars count in:

Mix is filtered

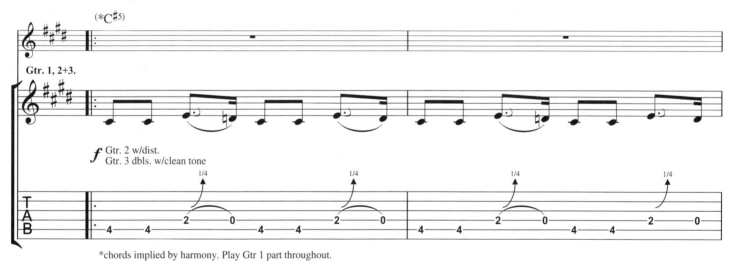

*chords implied by harmony. Play Gtr 1 part throughout.

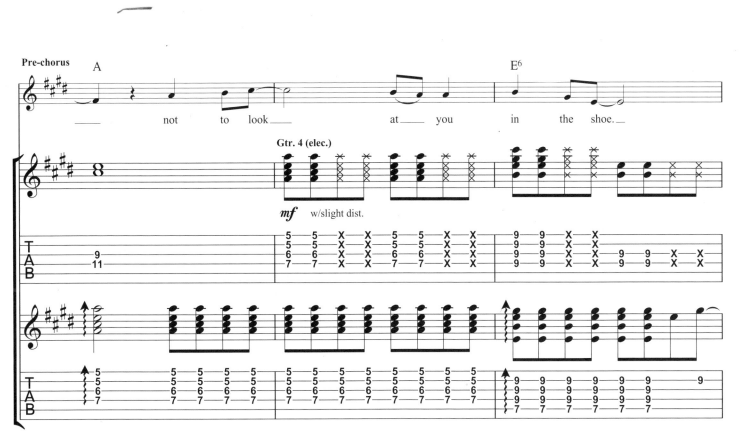

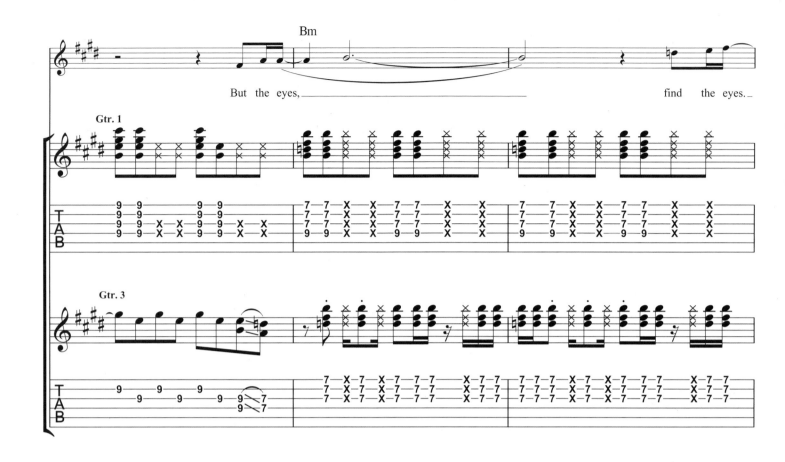

But the eyes,_____ find the eyes._

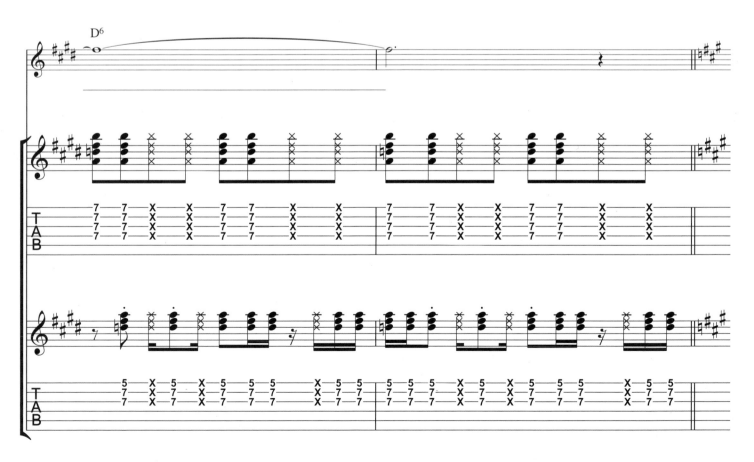

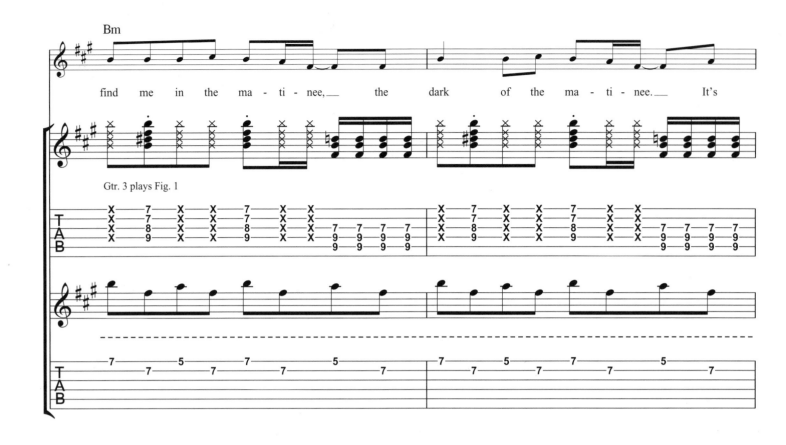

find me in the ma - ti - nee,___ the dark of the ma - ti - nee.___ It's

Gtr. 3 plays Fig. 1

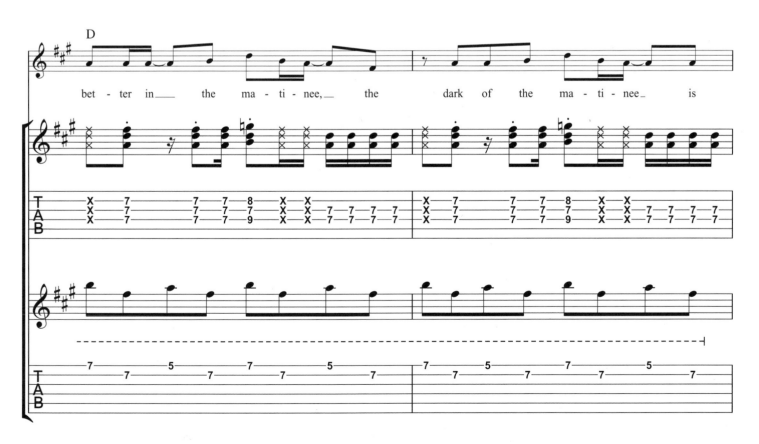

bet - ter in___ the ma - ti - nee,___ the dark of the ma - ti - nee___ is

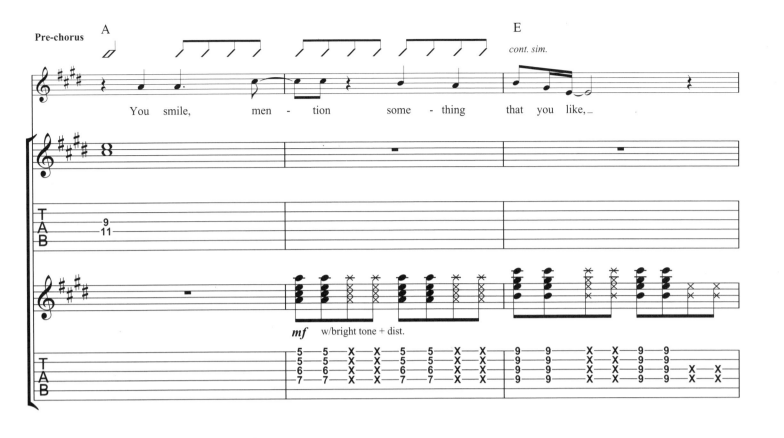

You smile, men - tion some - thing that you like,

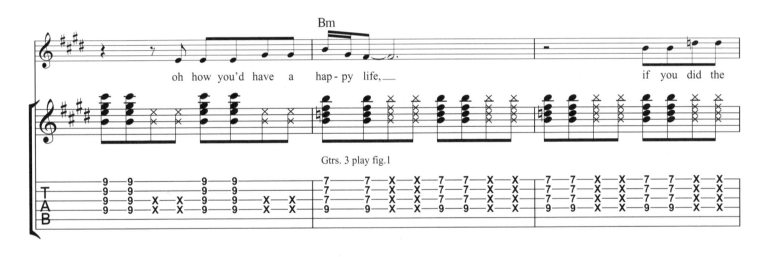

oh how you'd have a hap - py life, ___ if you did the

Gtrs. 3 play fig.1

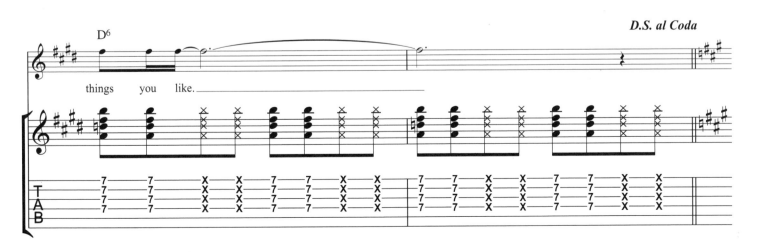

things you like.

D.S. al Coda

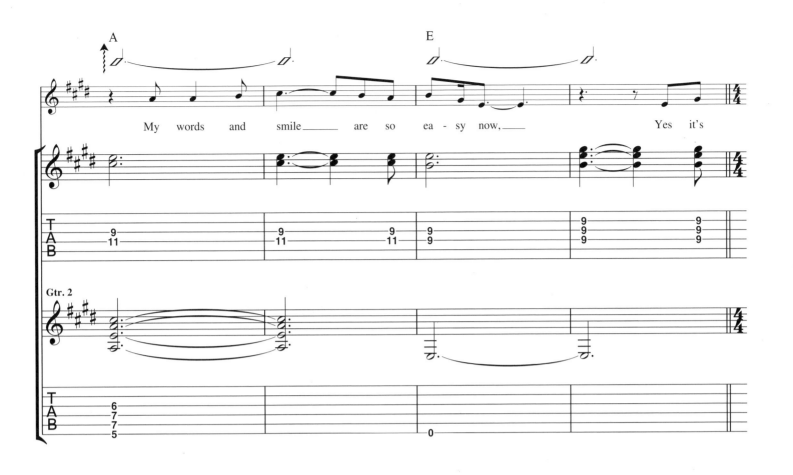

My words and smile____ are so ea - sy now,____ Yes it's

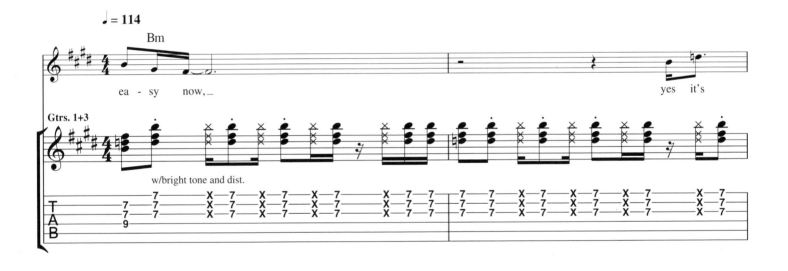

♩ = 114

ea - sy now,____ yes it's

w/bright tone and dist.

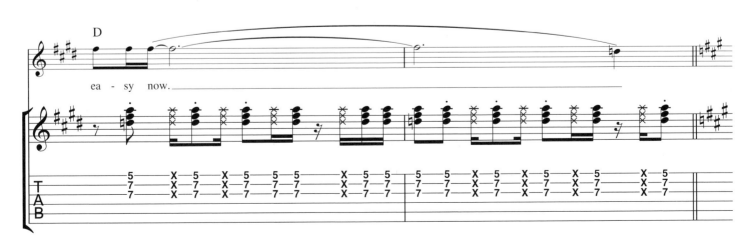

ea - sy now.____

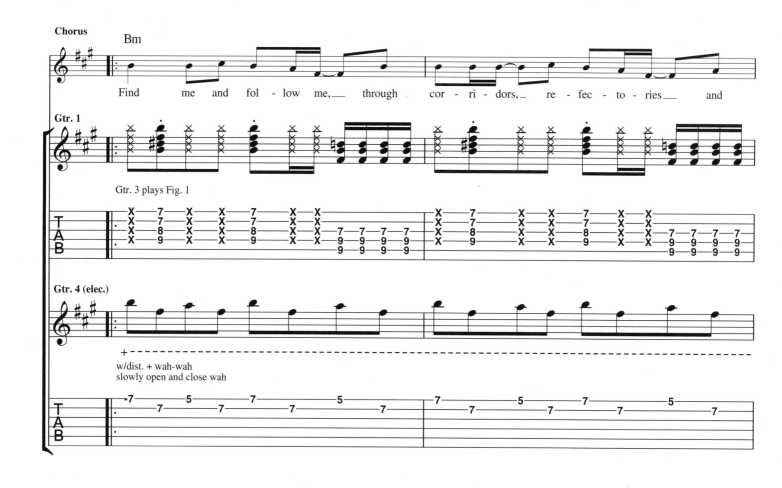

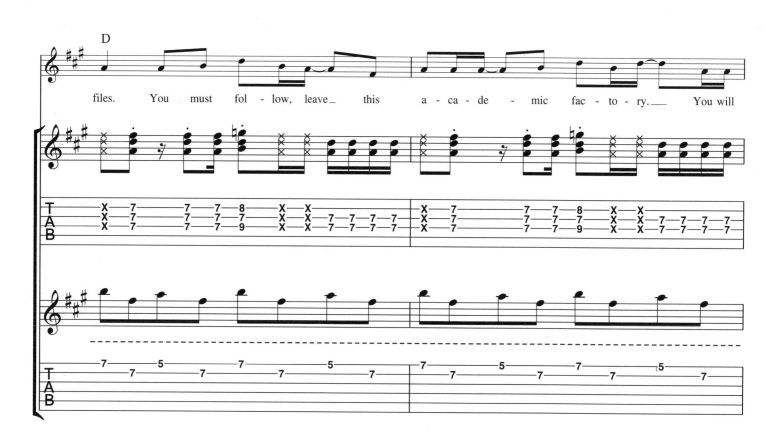

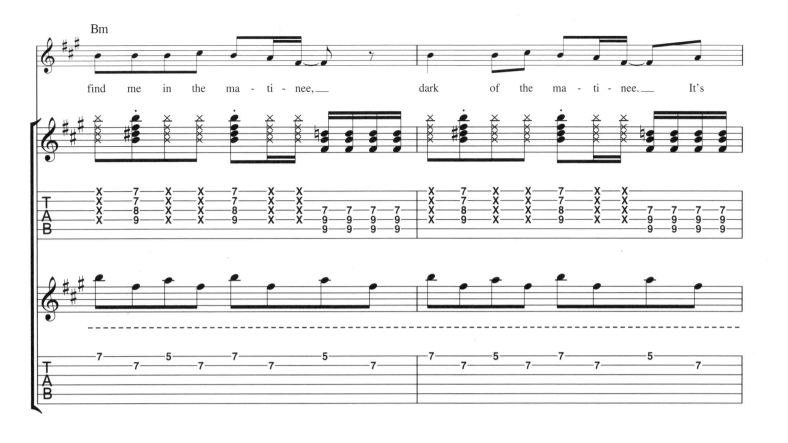

find me in the ma - ti - nee,___ dark of the ma - ti - nee.___ It's

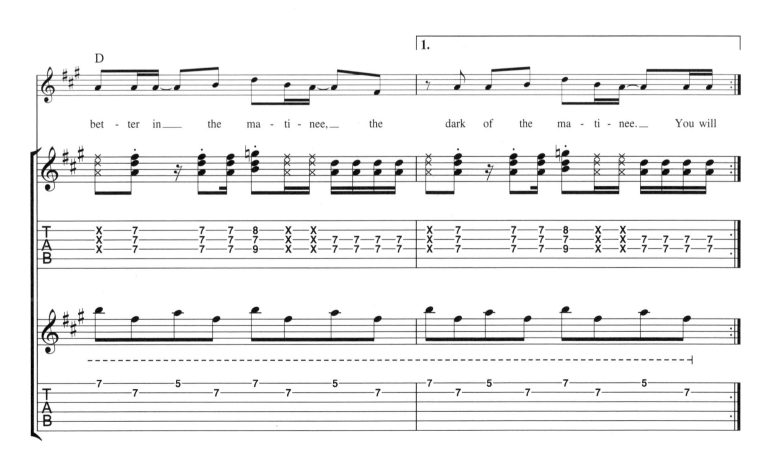

bet - ter in___ the ma - ti - nee,___ the dark of the ma - ti - nee.___ You will

auf achse

Words & Music by Alexander Kapranos & Nicholas McCarthy

2 bars count in:

♩ = 124

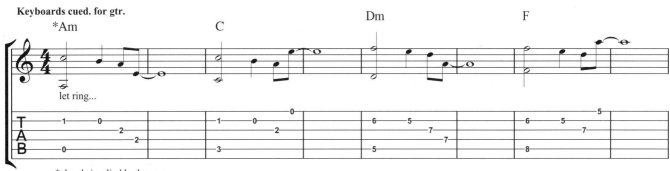

*chords implied by harmony

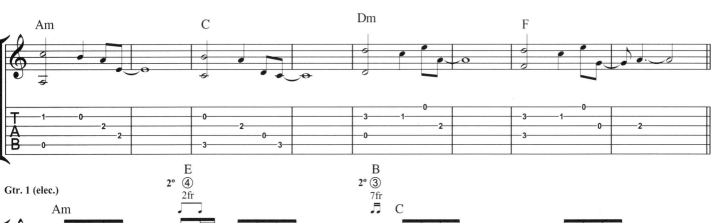

Gtr. 1 (elec.)

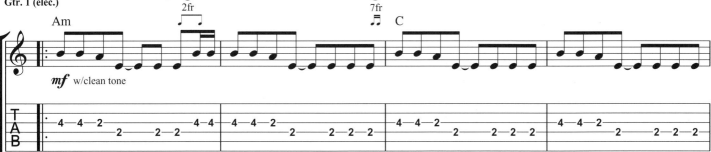

Play written part throughout

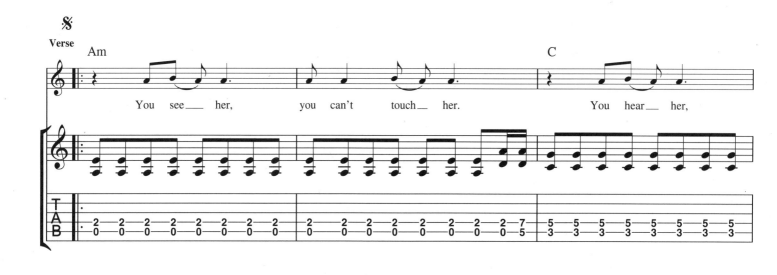

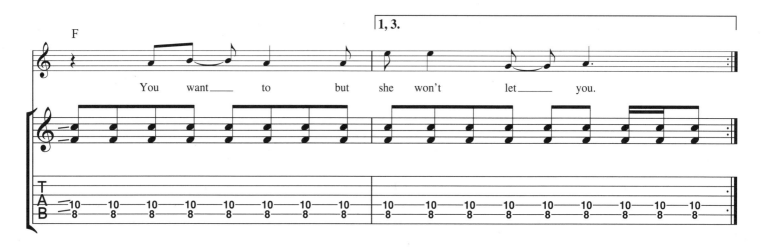

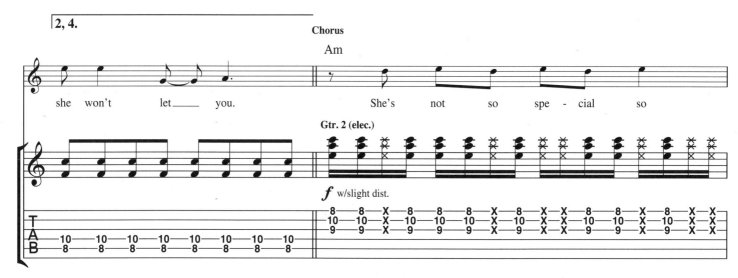

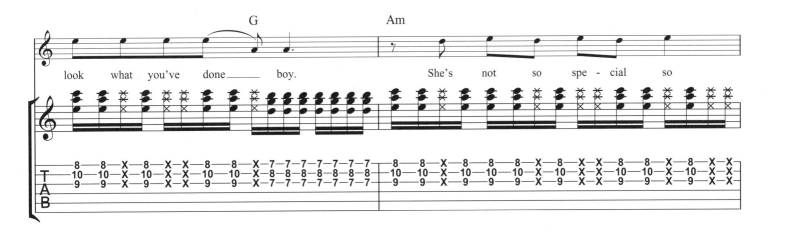

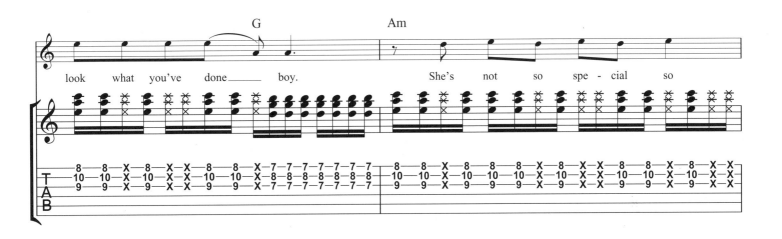

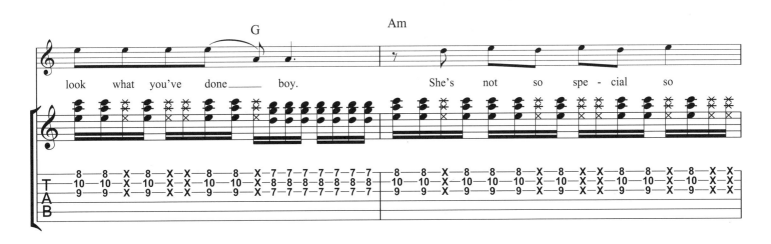

To Coda ⊕

Bridge

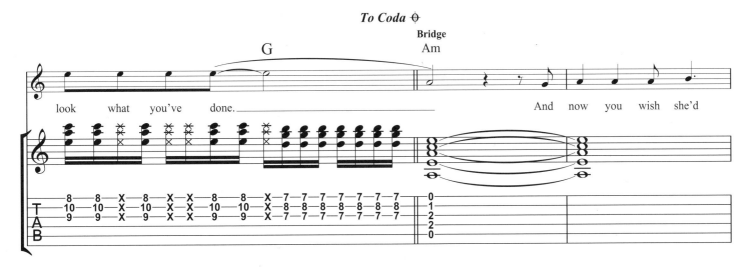

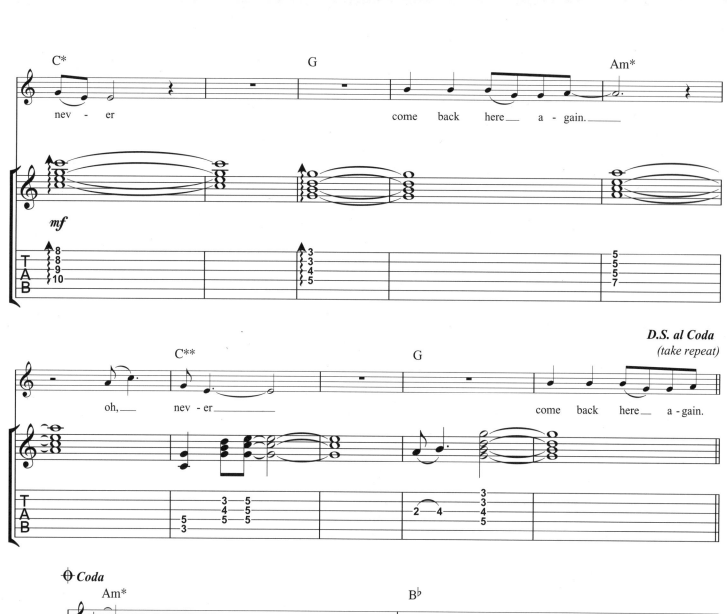

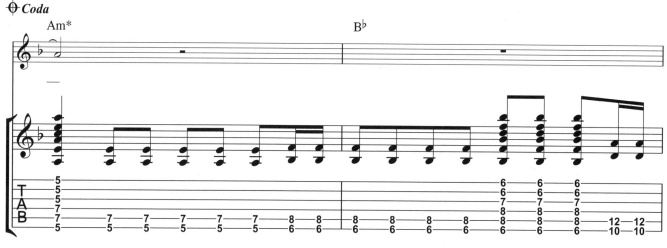

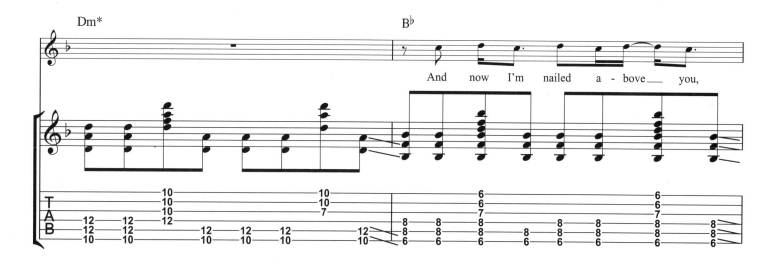

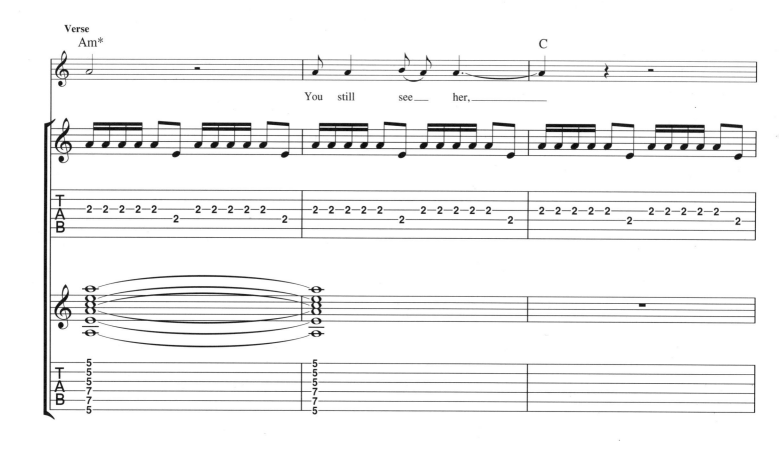

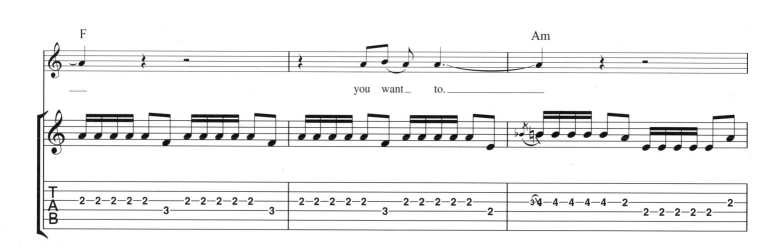

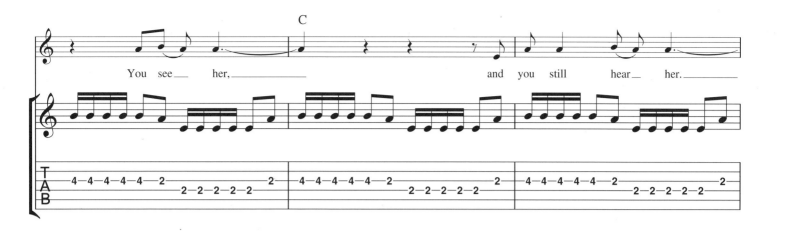

You see___ her,_____ and you still hear___ her._____

You want___ her,_____ and

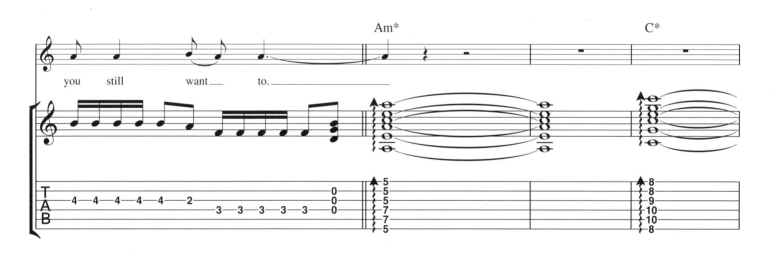

you still want___ to._____

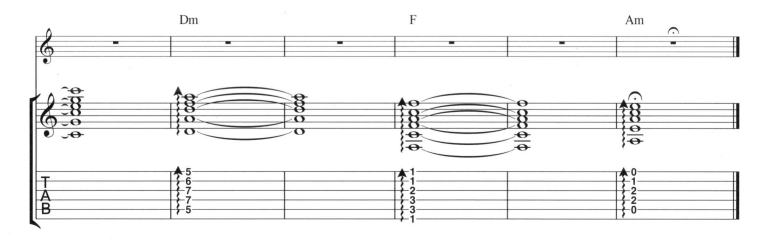

this fire

Words & Music by Alexander Kapranos & Nicholas McCarthy

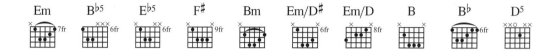

Em   B♭5   E♭5   F#   Bm   Em/D#   Em/D   B   B♭   D5

2 bars count in:

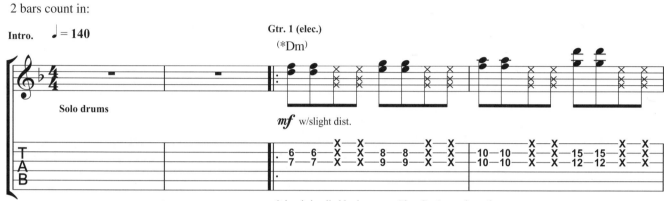

Intro. ♩ = 140

Gtr. 1 (elec.)

(*Dm)

Solo drums

mf w/slight dist.

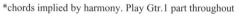

*chords implied by harmony. Play Gtr.1 part throughout

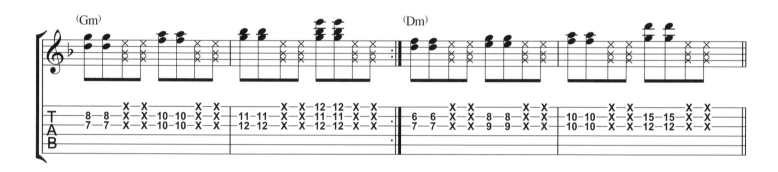

(Gm)   (Dm)

𝄋 Verse

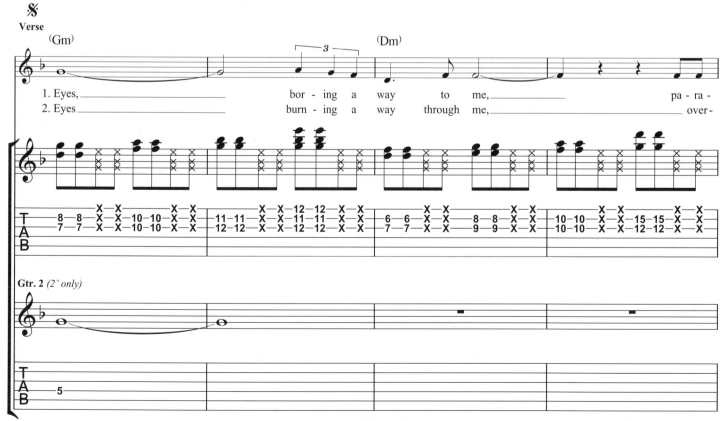

(Gm)   (Dm)

1. Eyes, _____ bor - ing a way to me, _____ pa - ra -
2. Eyes _____ burn - ing a way through me, _____ over-

Gtr. 2 (2° only)

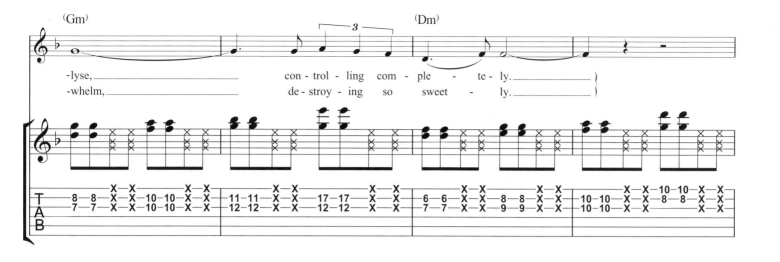

Pre-chorus

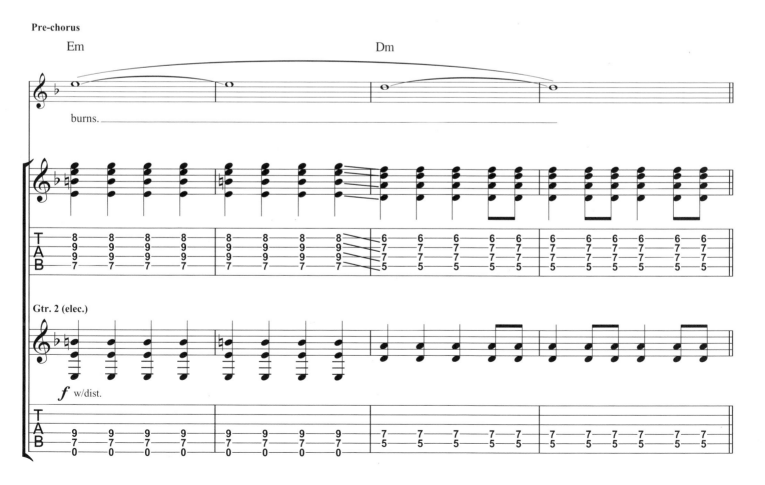

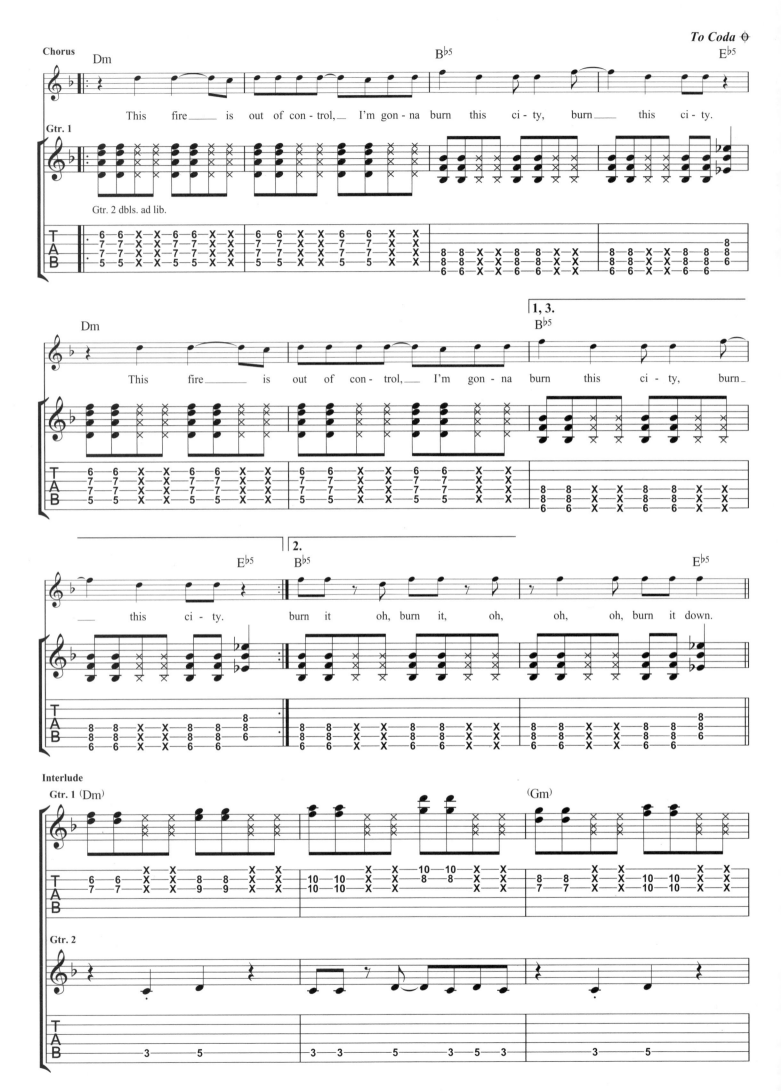

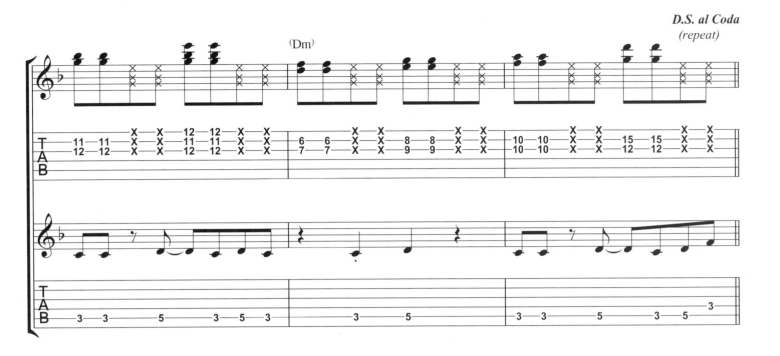

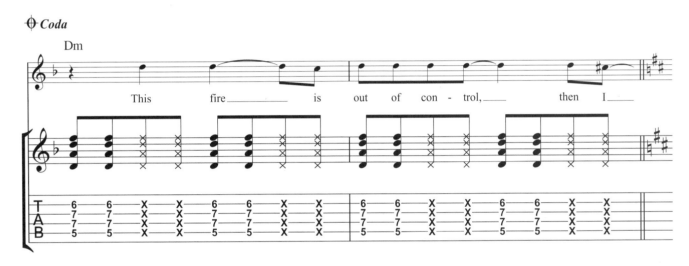

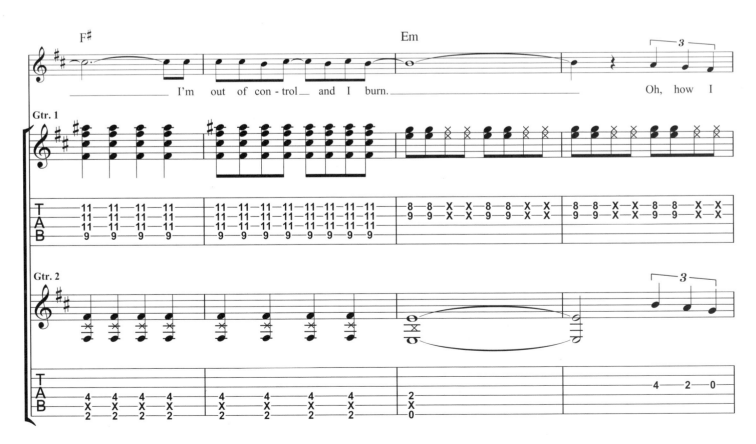

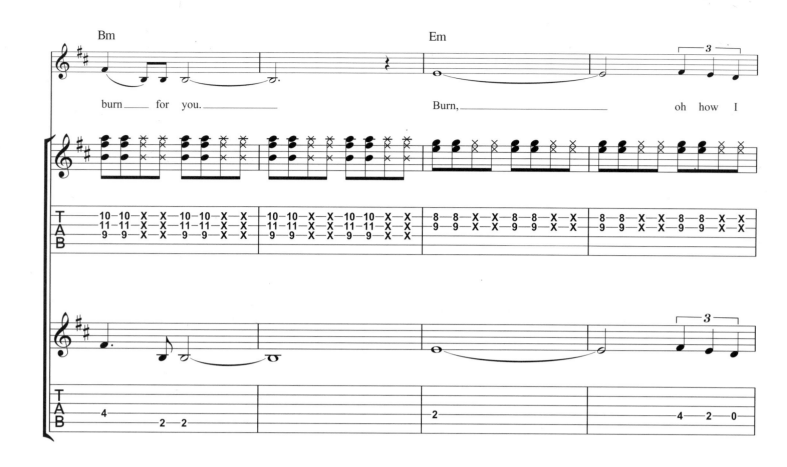

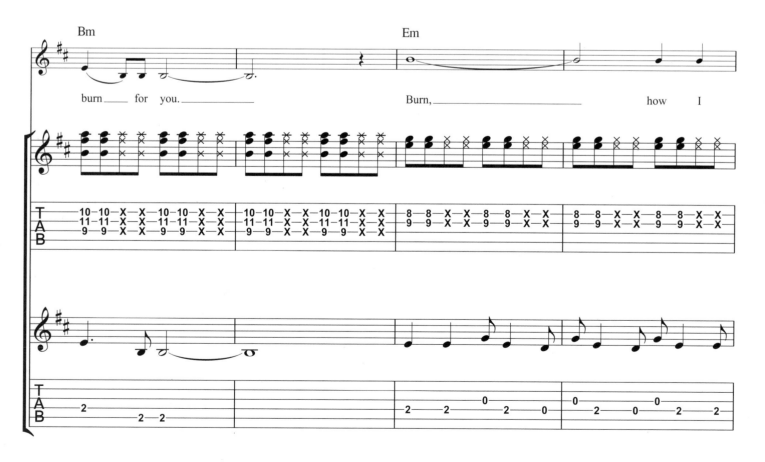

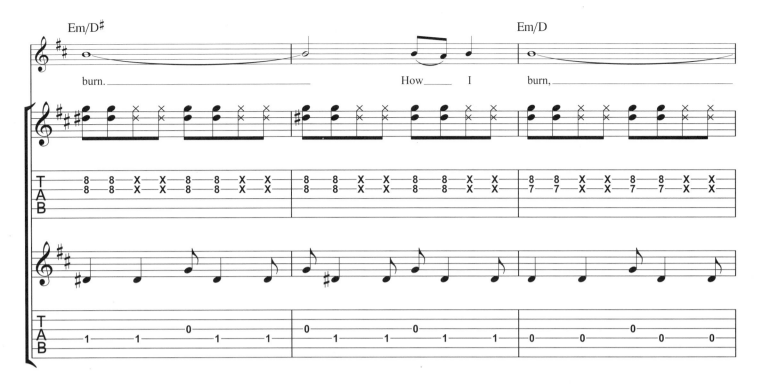

burn. _____ How ___ I ___ burn,

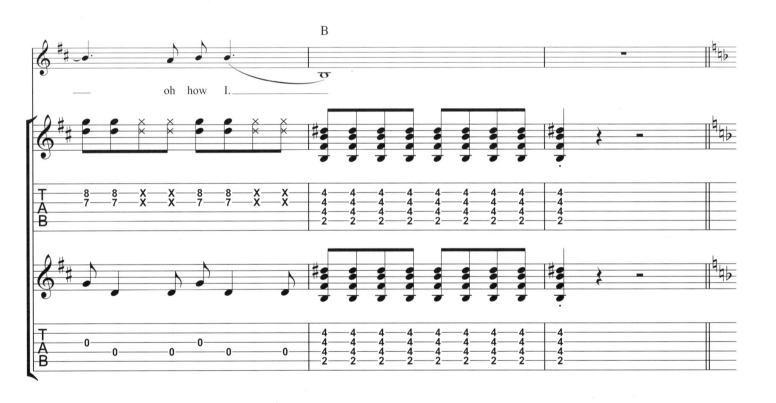

— oh how I. _____

Interlude

Gtr. 1 (Dm)   (Gm)

Gtr. 2 tacet

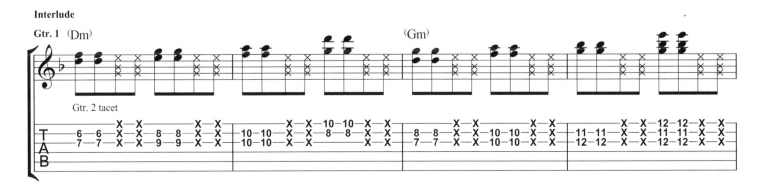

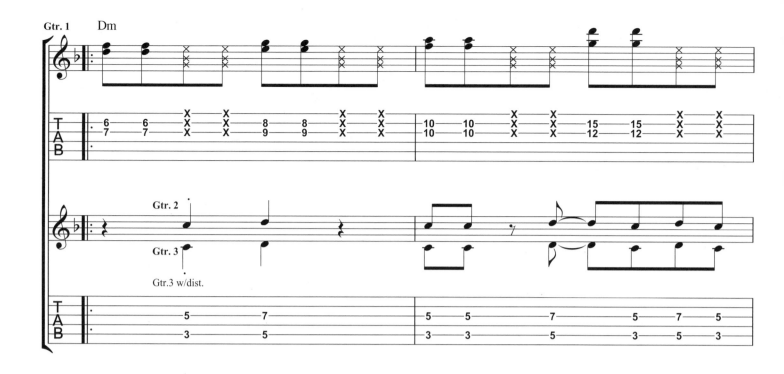

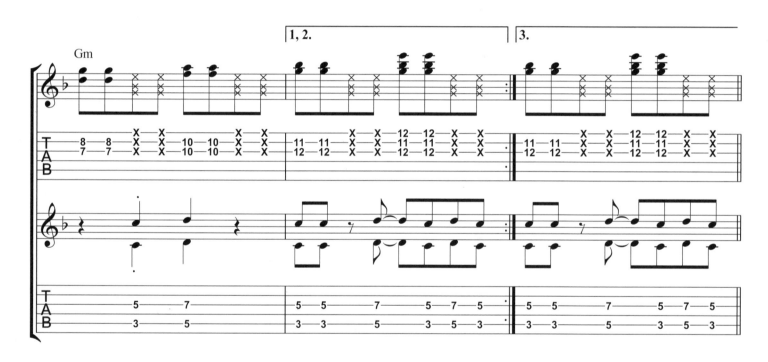

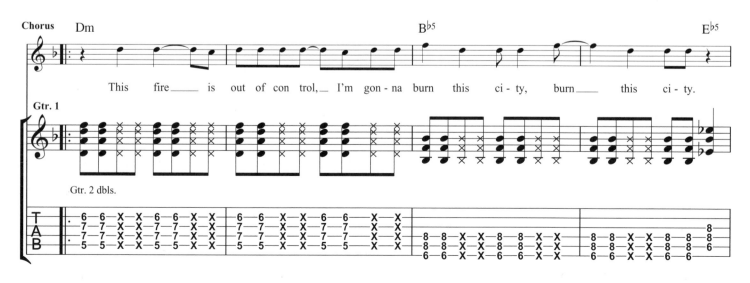

The lyrics in the chorus read: This fire is out of control, I'm gon-na burn this ci-ty, burn this ci-ty.

darts of pleasure

Words & Music by Alexander Kapranos & Nicholas McCarthy

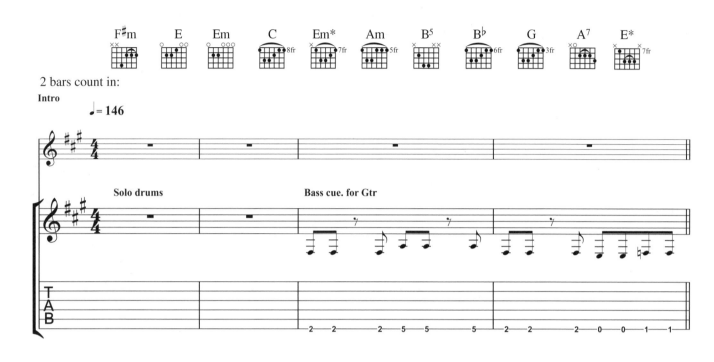

2 bars count in:

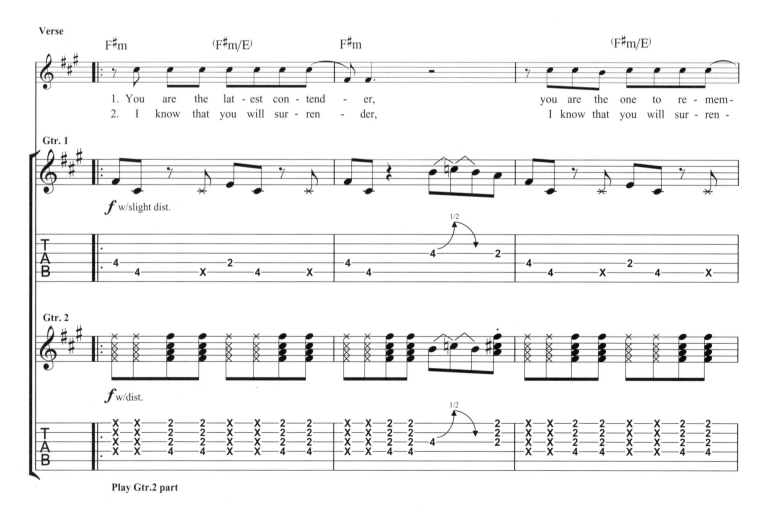

Play Gtr.2 part

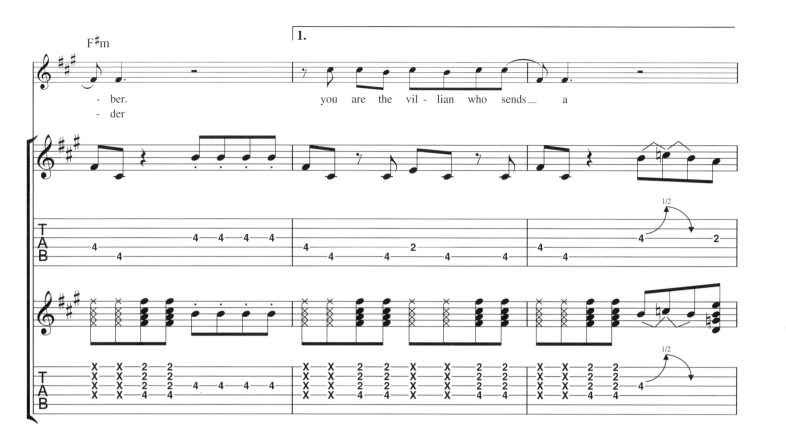

-ber. you are the vil - lian who sends___ a
-der

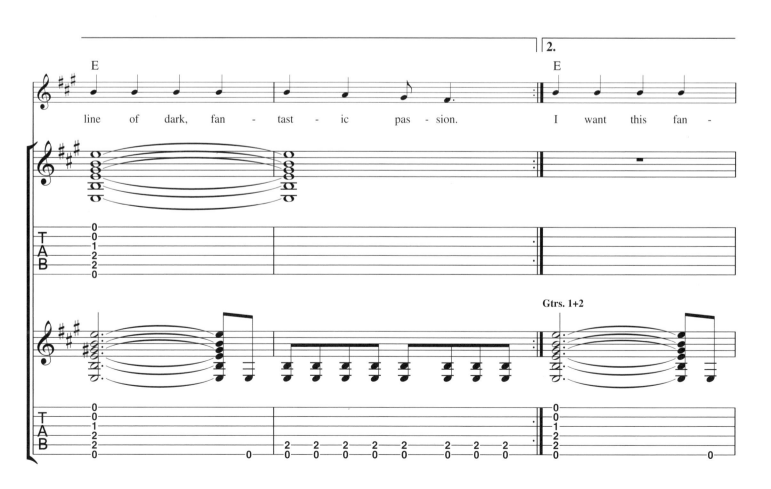

line of dark, fan - tast - ic pas - sion.   I want this fan -

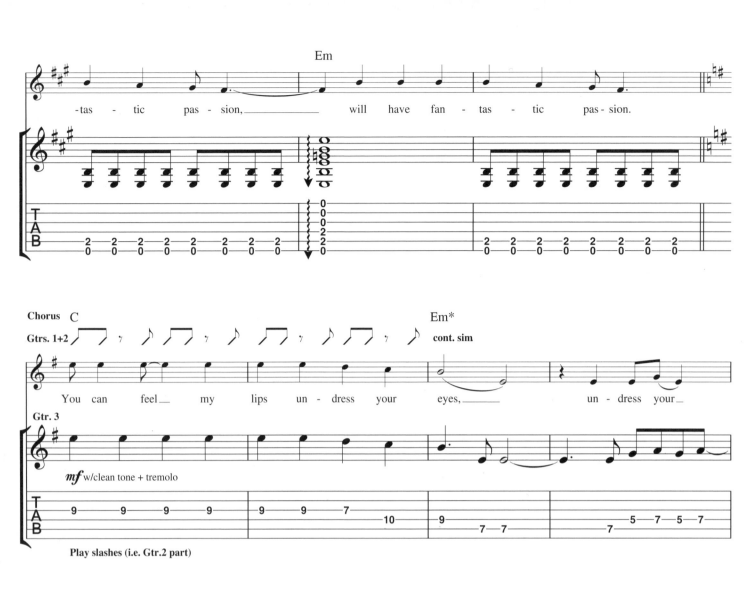

-tas - tic pas - sion,_____ will have fan - tas - tic pas - sion.

Chorus C

Gtrs. 1+2   cont. sim

Em*

You can feel___ my lips un - dress your eyes,_____ un - dress your___

Gtr. 3

mf w/clean tone + tremolo

Play slashes (i.e. Gtr.2 part)

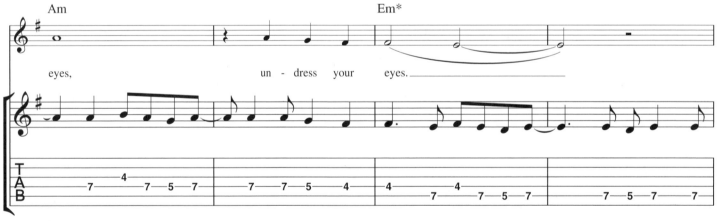

Am   Em*

eyes,   un - dress your eyes._____

C   Em*

Words of love___ and words so lei - sured, words are poi - soned darts of plea - sure,

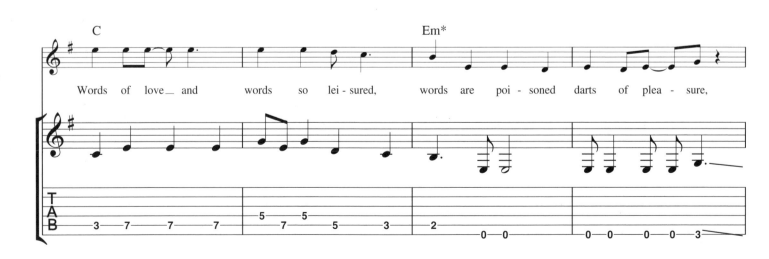

die,_____ and so you die._____

3. You are the lat-est ad-vent-ure,   I____
4. I know that you will sur-ren-der,

you're an e-mo-tion a-veng-er,   you are the dev-il that sells___
_____ know that you will sur-ren - der

un - dress your eyes.

Skin can feel my lips, they tin - gle, tense an - ti - ci - pa - tion.

This one ___ is an ea - sy one, ___ feel ___ the word ___ and melt up - on it.

63

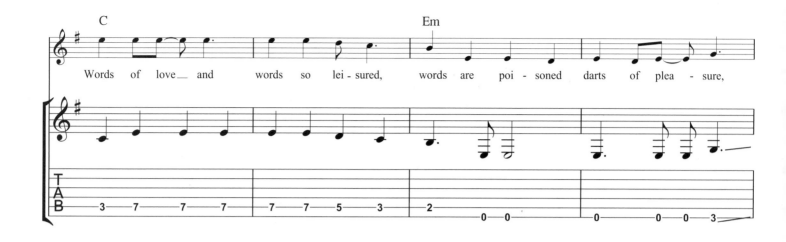

Words of love and words so lei - sured, words are poi - soned darts of plea - sure,

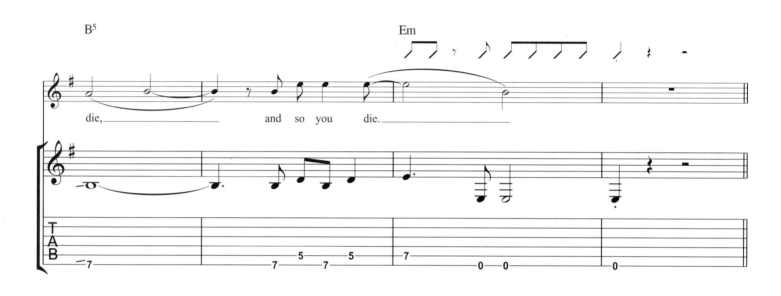

die, and so you die.

Interlude

Bass arr. for gtr

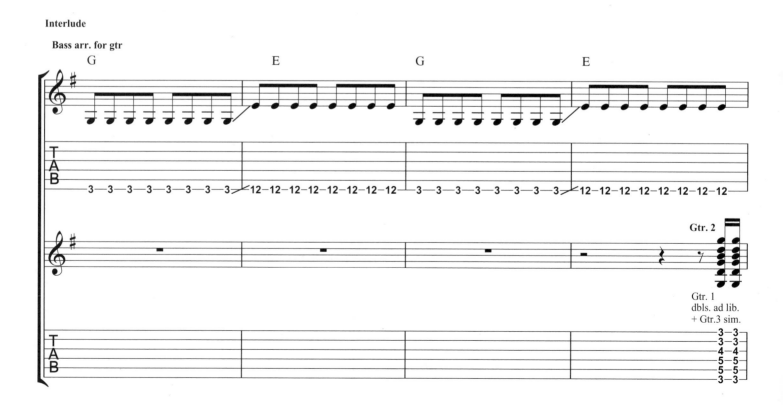

Gtr. 1
dbls. ad lib.
+ Gtr.3 sim.

cheating on you

Words & Music by Alexander Kapranos & Nicholas McCarthy

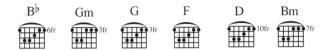

2 bars count in:

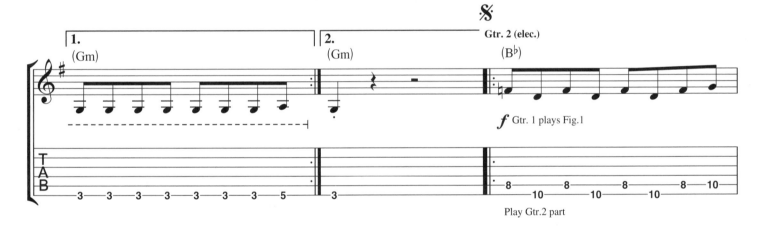

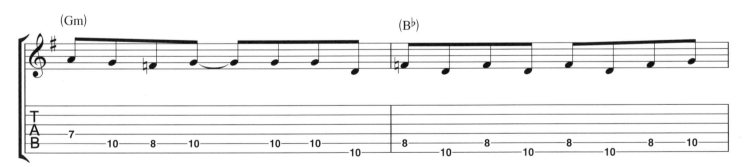

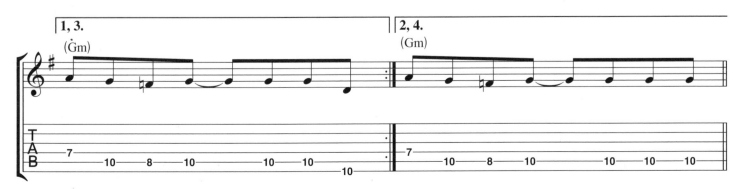

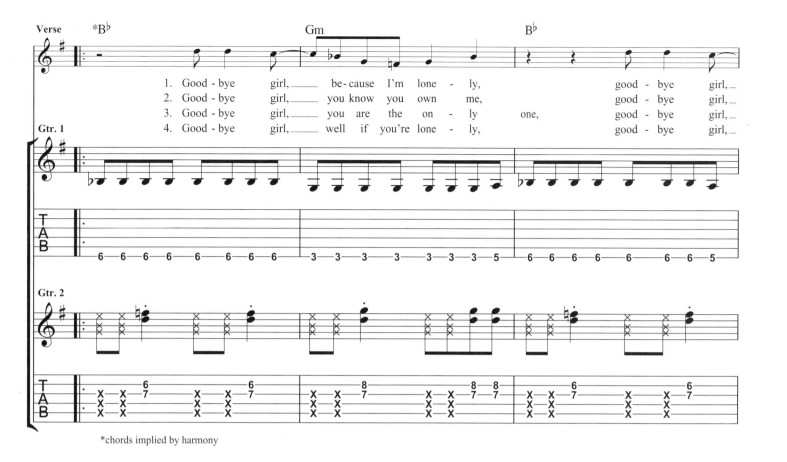

1. Good - bye girl,___ be - cause I'm lone - ly, good - bye girl,___
2. Good - bye girl,___ you know you own me, good - bye girl,___
3. Good - bye girl,___ you are the on - ly one, good - bye girl,___
4. Good - bye girl,___ well if you're lone - ly, good - bye girl,___

*chords implied by harmony

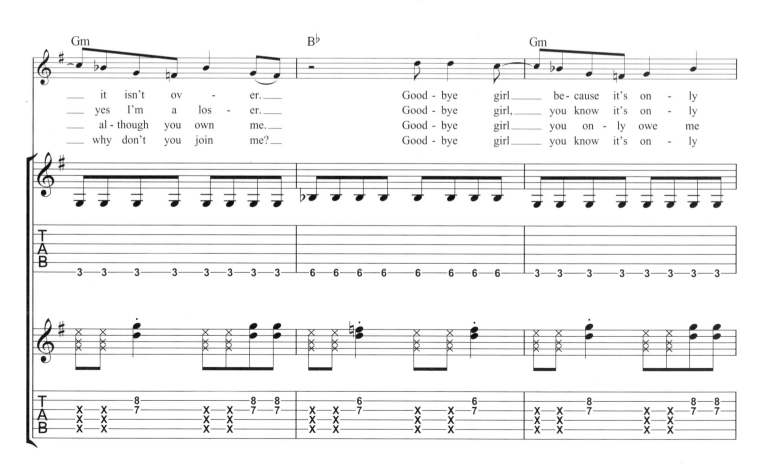

___ it isn't ov - er.___ Good - bye girl___ be - cause it's on - ly
___ yes I'm a los - er.___ Good - bye girl, you know it's on - ly
___ al - though you own me.___ Good - bye girl you on - ly owe me
why don't you join me?___ Good - bye girl you know it's on - ly

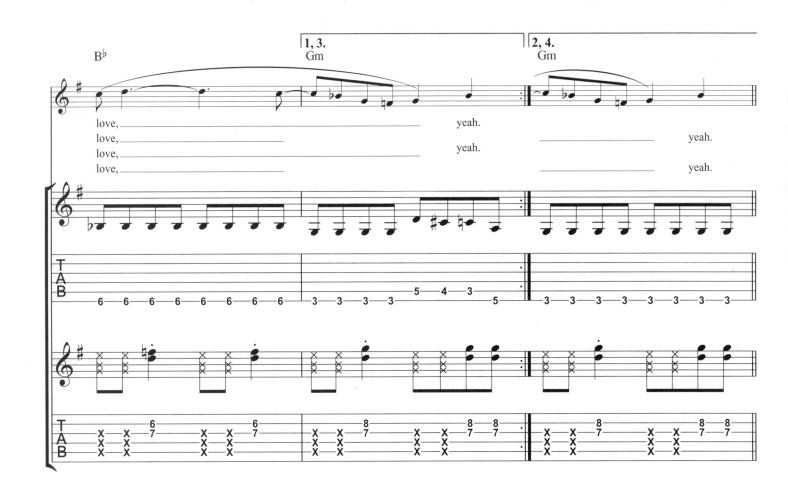

love, _____ yeah.
love, _____ yeah.
love, _____ yeah.
love, _____ yeah.

Chorus

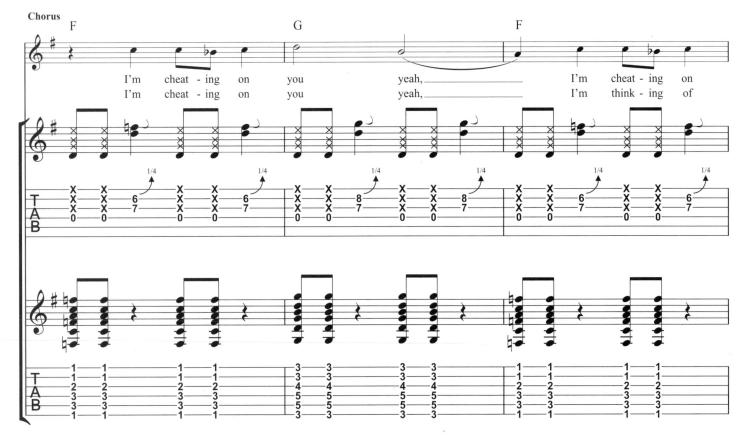

I'm cheat - ing on you yeah, _____ I'm cheat - ing on
I'm cheat - ing on you yeah, _____ I'm think - ing of

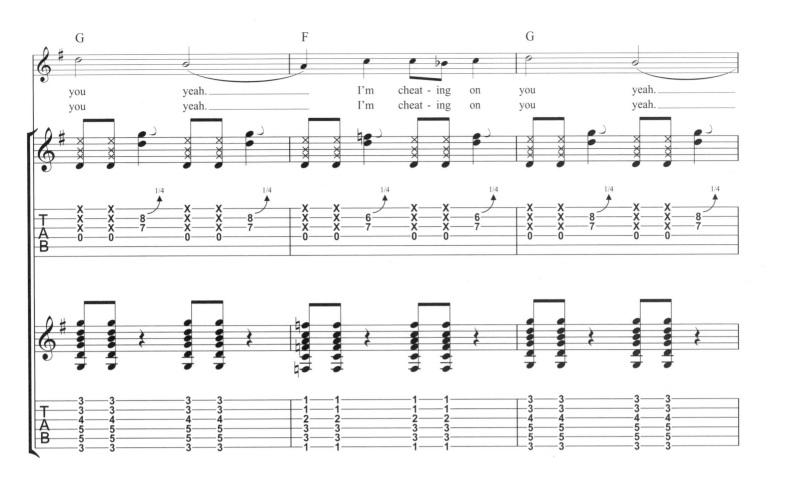

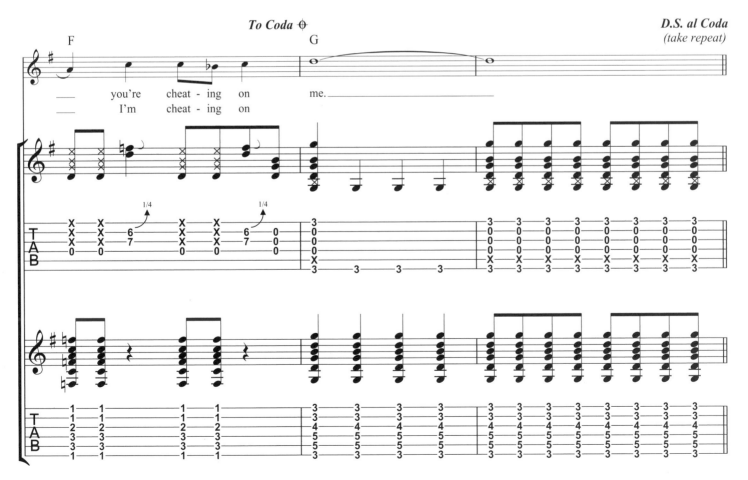

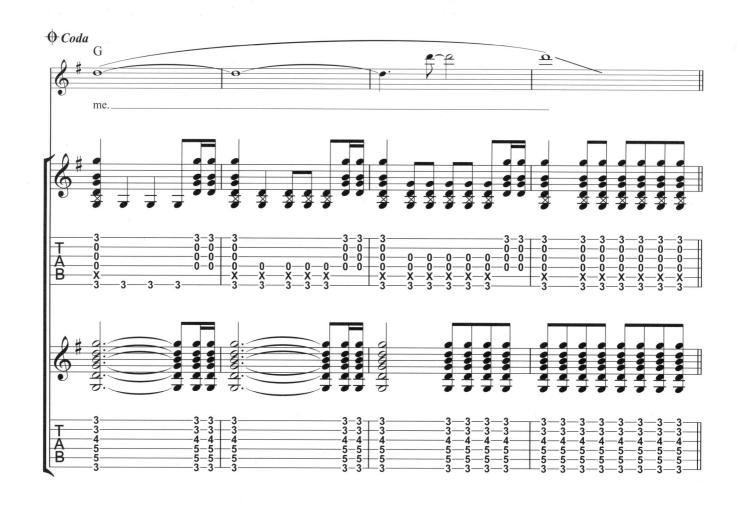

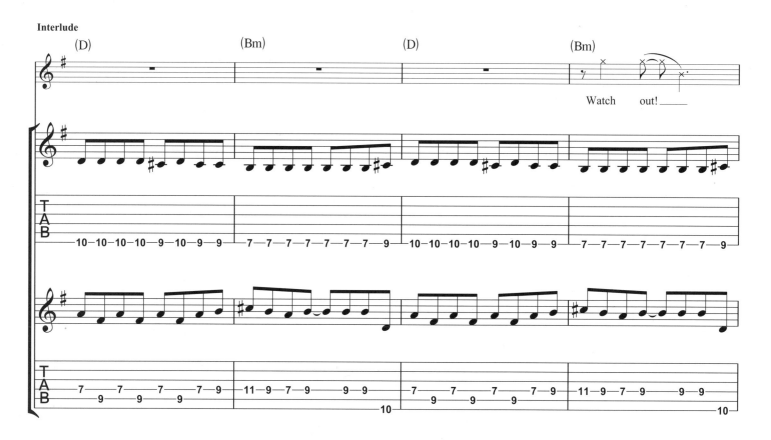

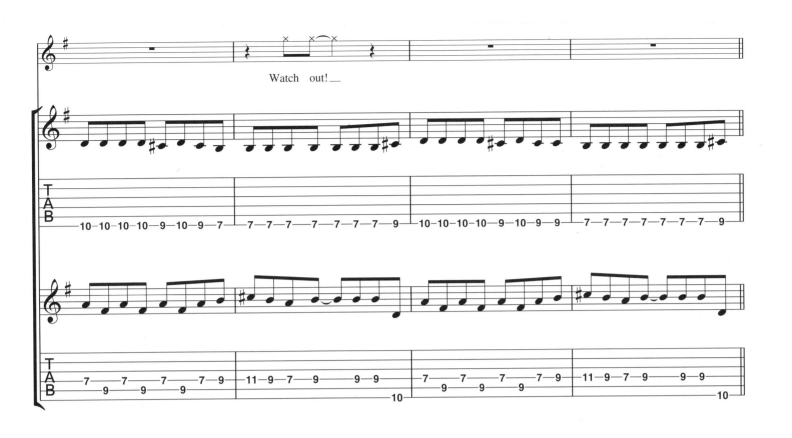

Watch out!—

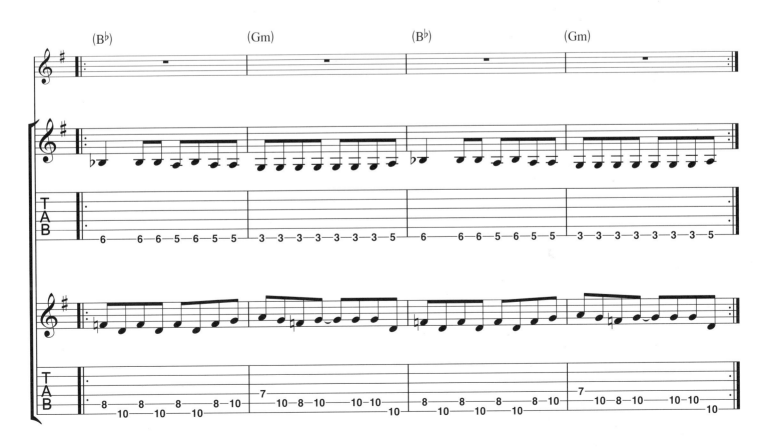

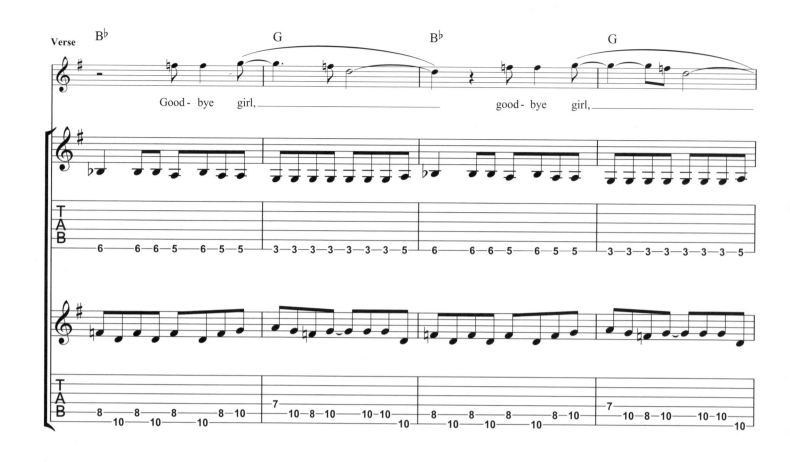

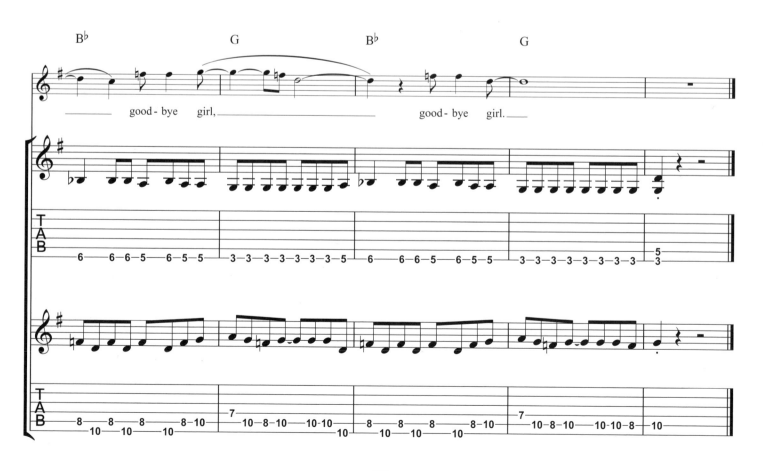

michael

Words & Music by Alexander Kapranos & Nicholas McCarthy

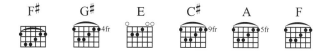

2 bars count in:

Intro. ♩ = 159

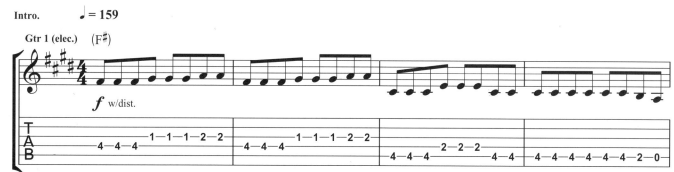

Play Gtr. 1 part throughout

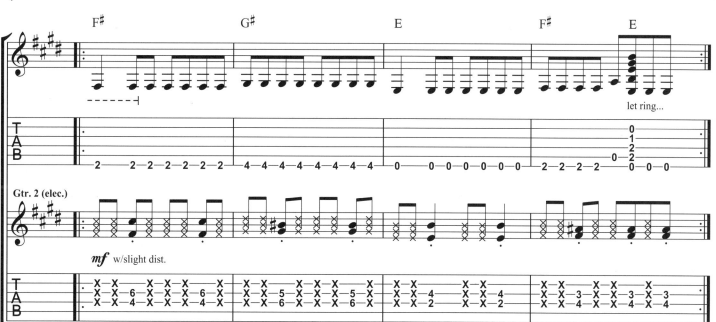

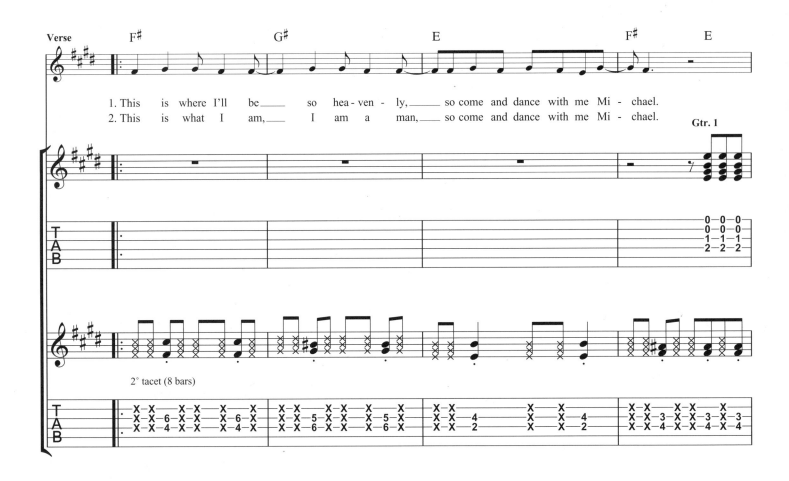

1. This is where I'll be____ so hea - ven - ly,____ so come and dance with me Mi - chael.
2. This is what I am,____ I am a man,____ so come and dance with me Mi - chael.

2° tacet (8 bars)

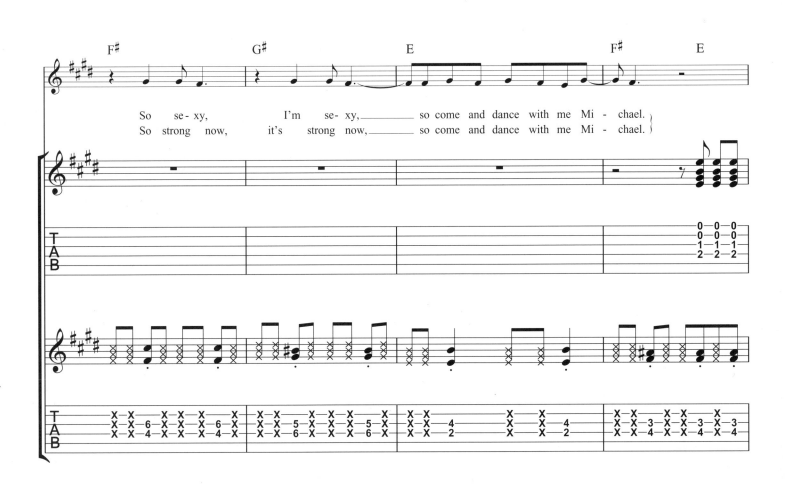

So se - xy,____ I'm se - xy,____ so come and dance with me Mi - chael.
So strong now,____ it's strong now,____ so come and dance with me Mi - chael.

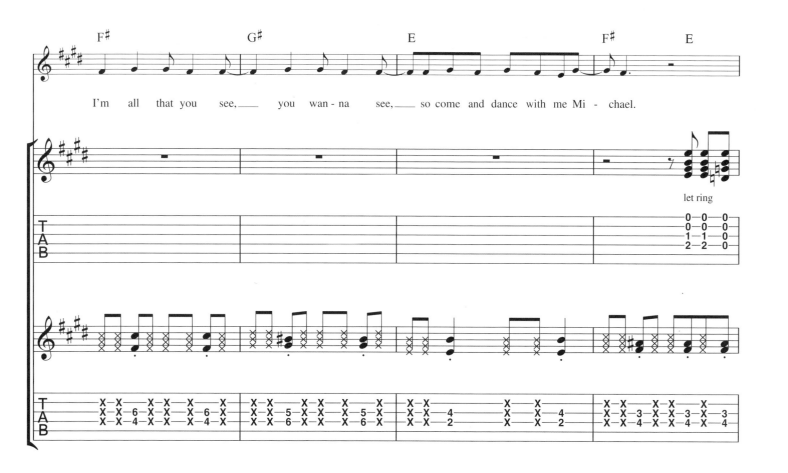

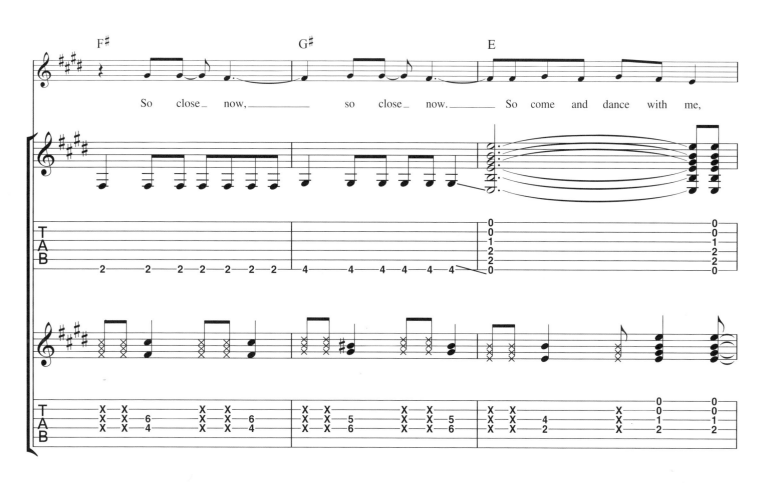

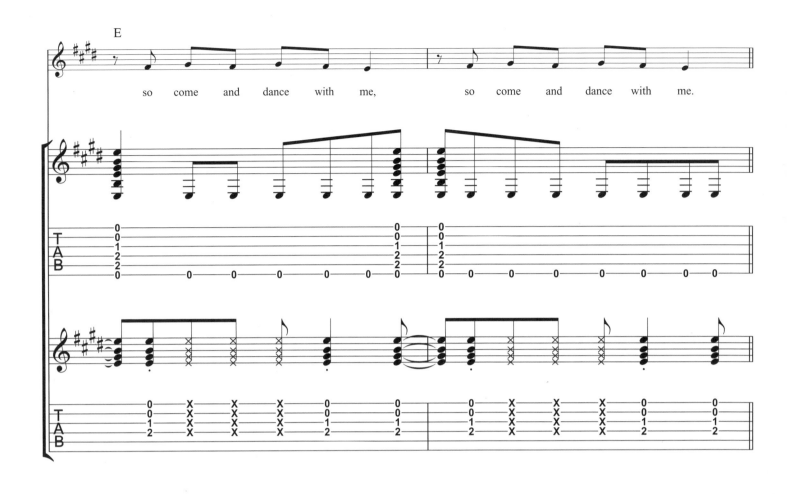

so come and dance with me, so come and dance with me.

%
Chorus

1. 2. Mi - chael, you're the boy___ with all the lea - ther hips, stick - y hair, stick - y hips, stub -
3. Mi - chael you're the on - ly one I'd ev - er want, on - ly one I'd ev - er want, on -

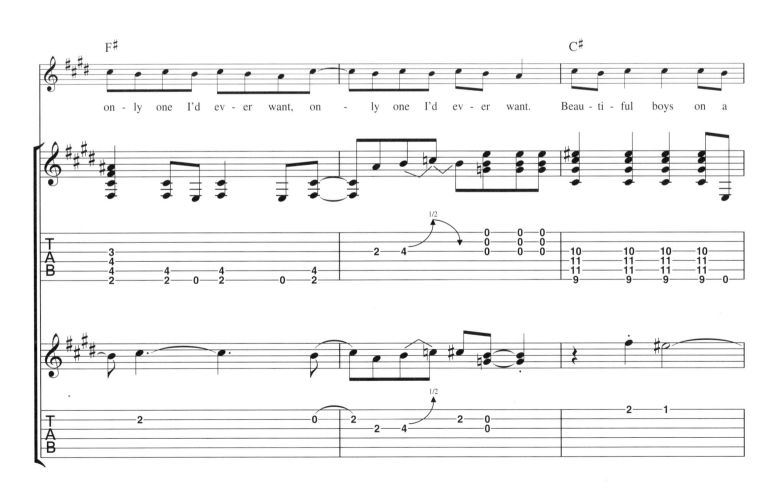

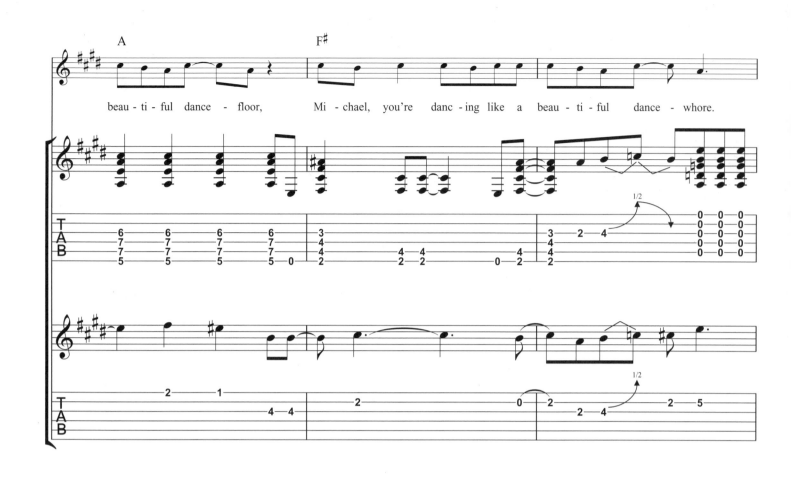

beau - ti - ful dance - floor, Mi - chael, you're danc - ing like a beau - ti - ful dance - whore.

Mi - chael wait - ing on a sil - ver plat - ter now, _____ and no - thing mat - ters now.

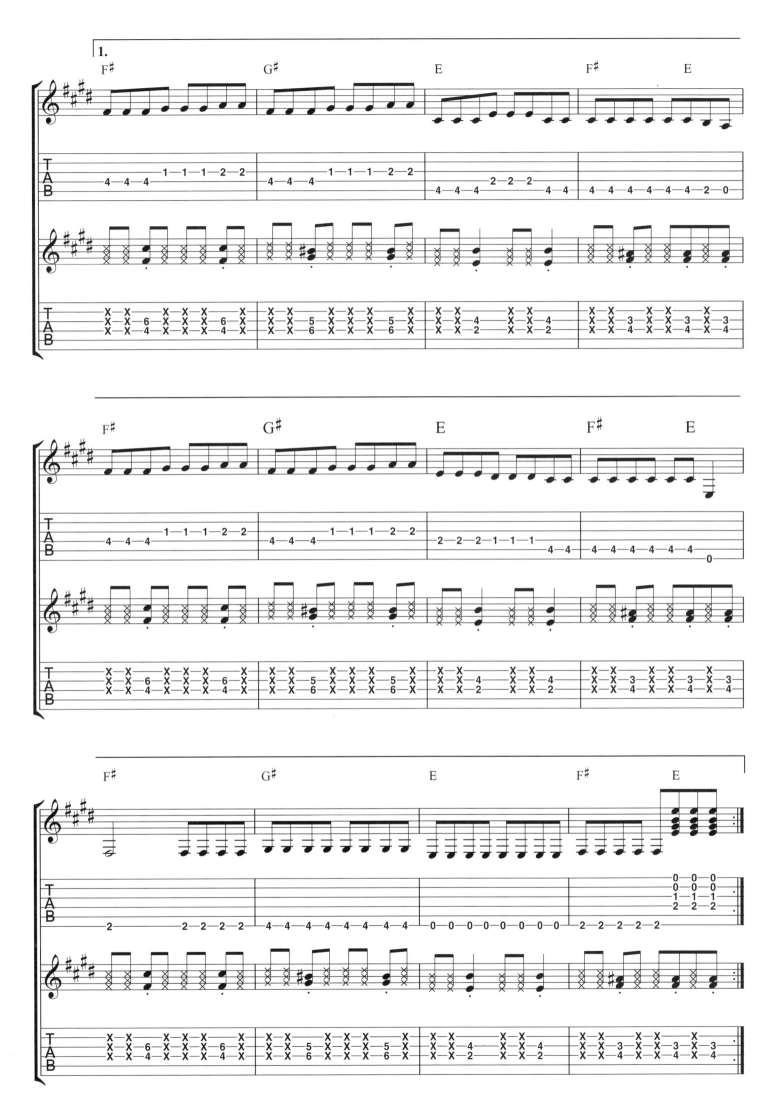

sil - ver plat - ter now, no - thing mat - ters now,

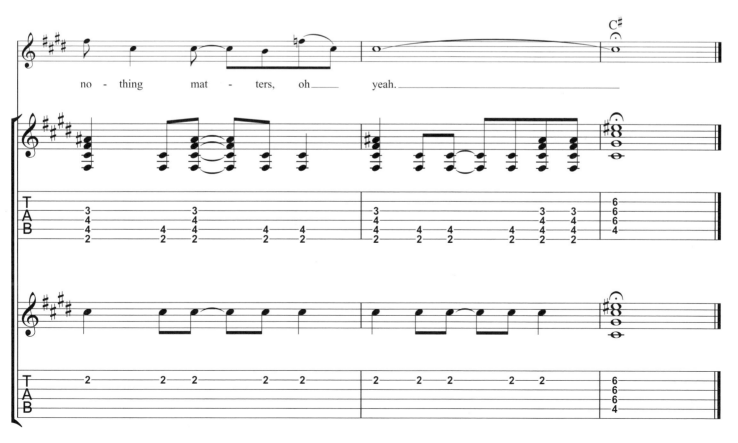

no - thing mat - ters, oh___ yeah.___

come on home

Words & Music by Alexander Kapranos & Nicholas McCarthy

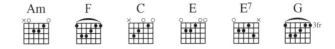

2 bars count in:

Intro. ♩ = 116

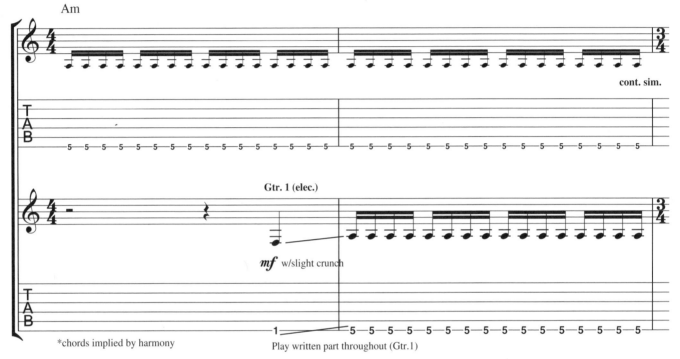

*chords implied by harmony

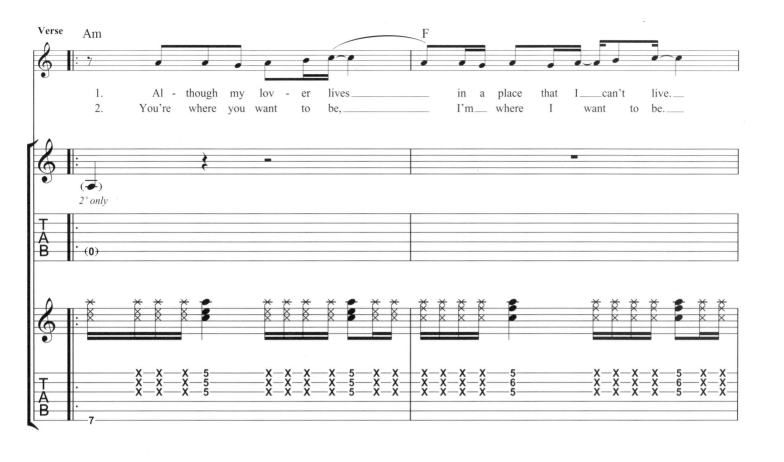

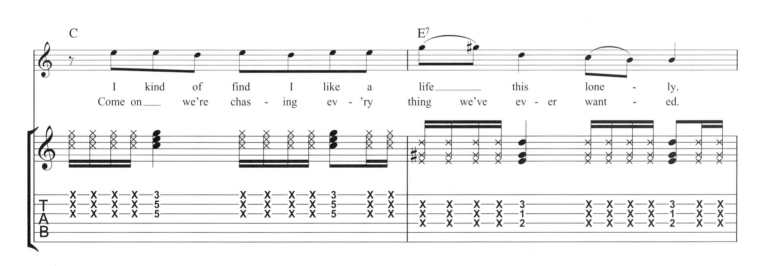

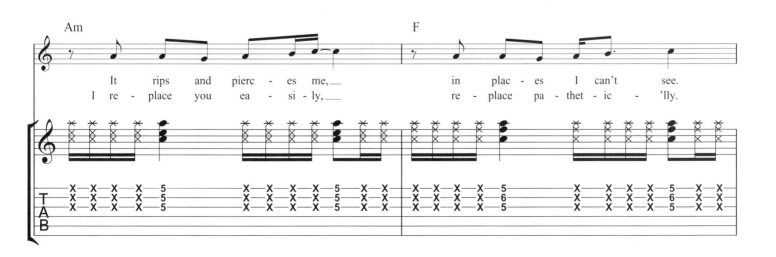

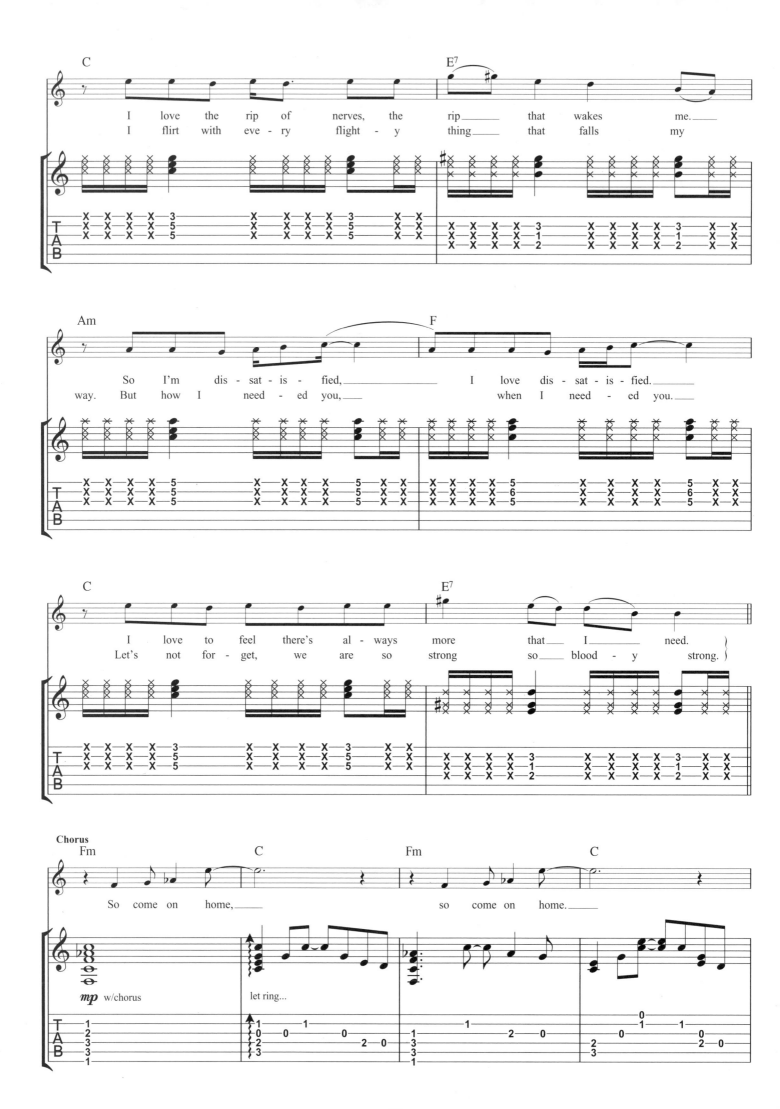

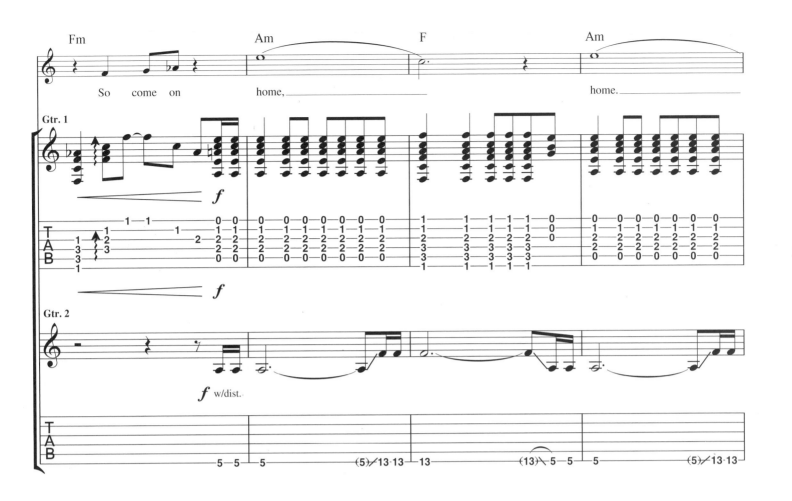

So come on home, home.

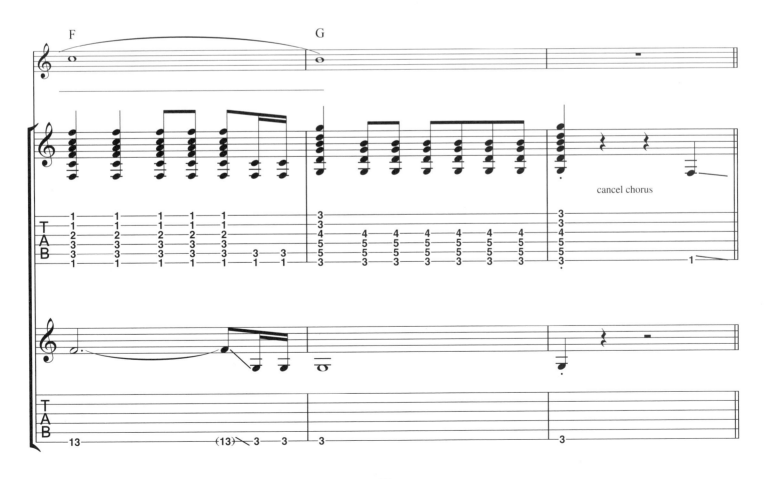

1. Interlude

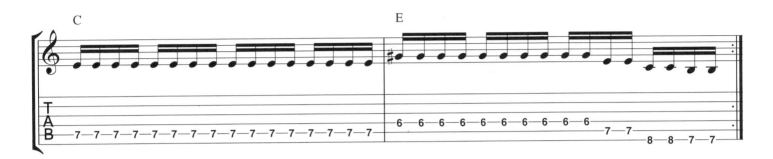

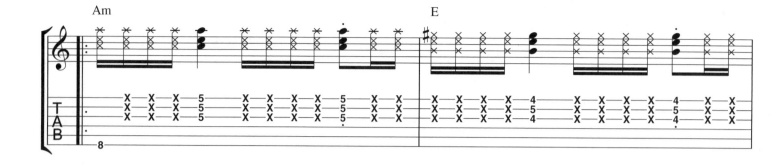

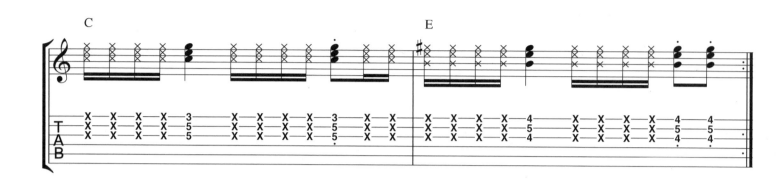

Bridge

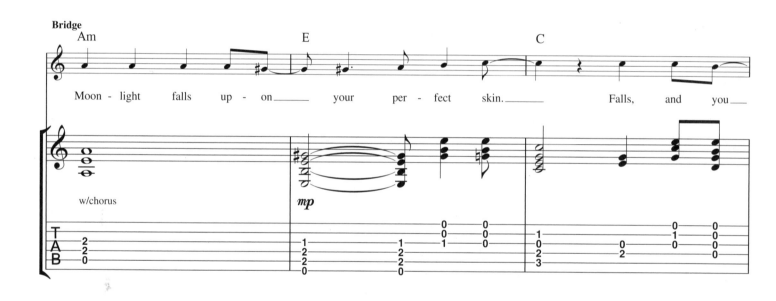

Moon - light falls up - on___ your per - fect skin.___ Falls, and you___

w/chorus

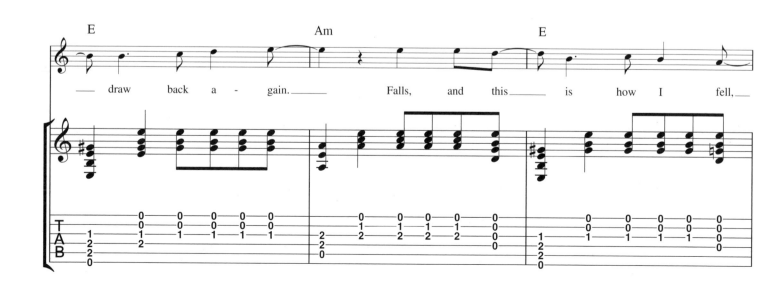

___ draw back a - gain.___ Falls, and this___ is how I fell,___

40'

Words & Music by Alexander Kapranos & Nicholas McCarthy

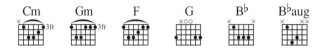

2 bars count in:

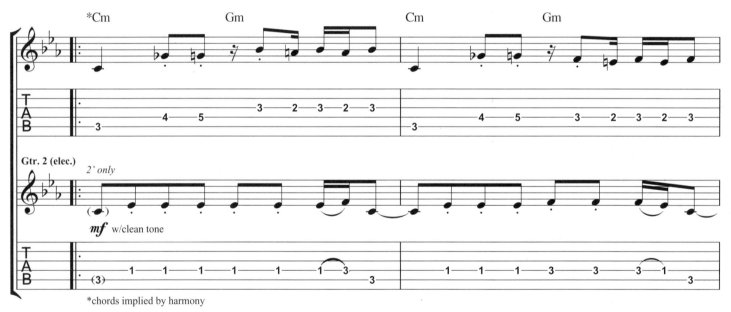

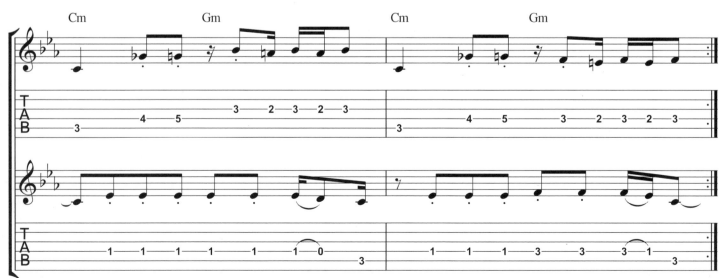

1. As I glance once up-on the foam, for-ty feet be-neath my
2. Salt scales up-on my dry-ing arms, burn my back be-neath the

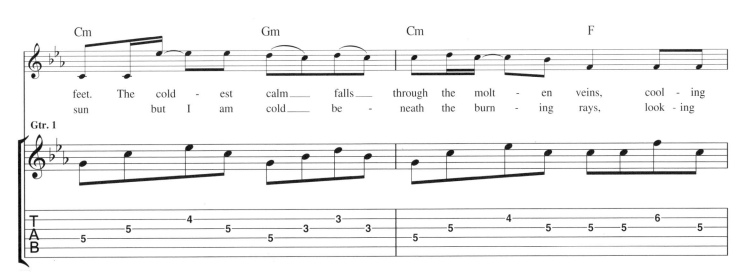

feet. The cold-est calm falls through the molt-en veins, cool-ing
sun but I am cold be-neath the burn-ing rays, look-ing

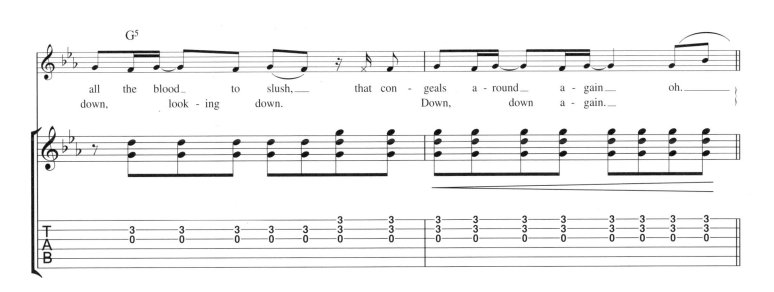

all the blood to slush, that con-geals a-round a-gain oh.
down, look-ing down. Down, down a-gain.

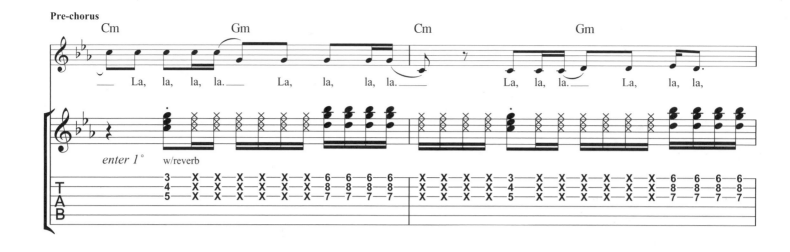

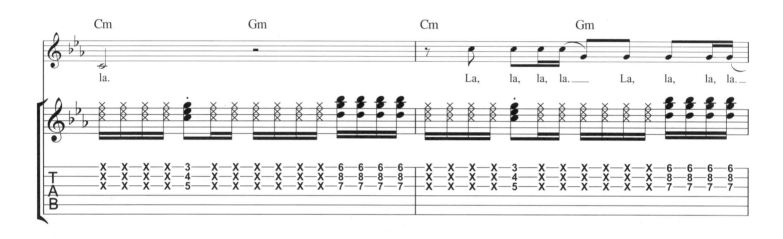

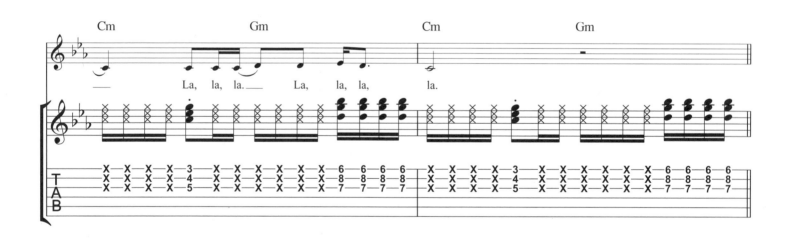

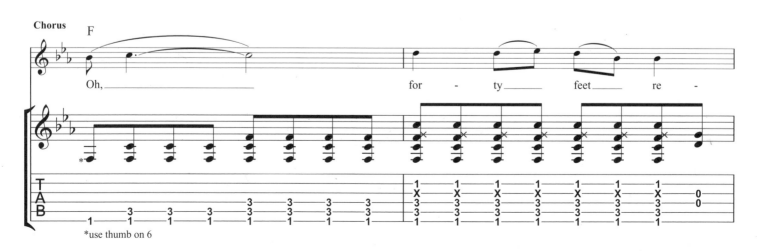

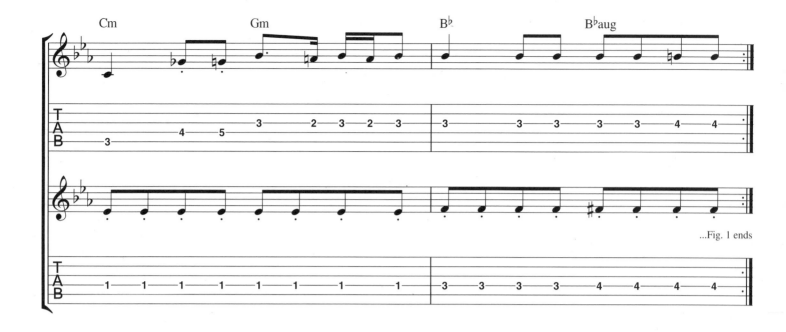

...Fig. 1 ends

Gtr. solo

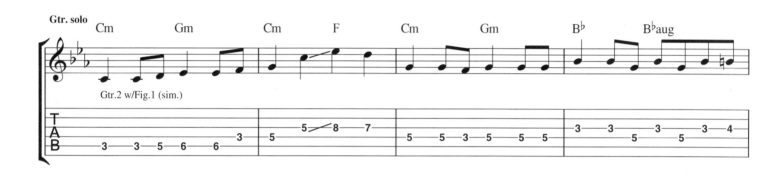

Gtr.2 w/Fig.1 (sim.)

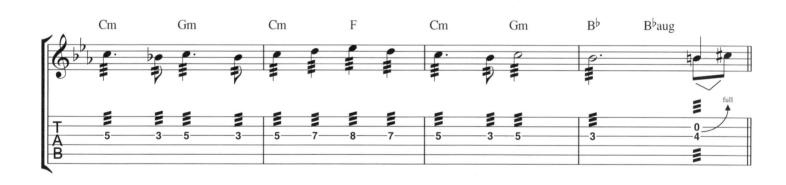

Pre-chorus

La, la, la, la. La, la, la, la. La, la, la. La, la, la, la.

Bass cue. for gtr.

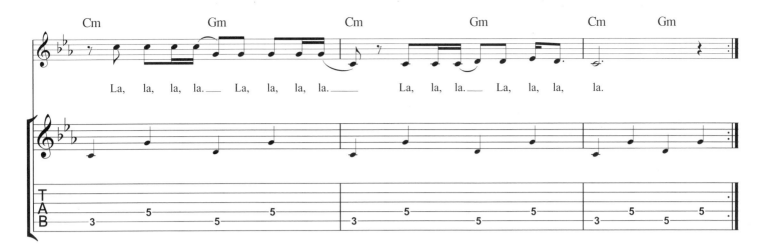

La, la, la, la. La, la, la, la. La, la, la. La, la, la, la.

Chorus

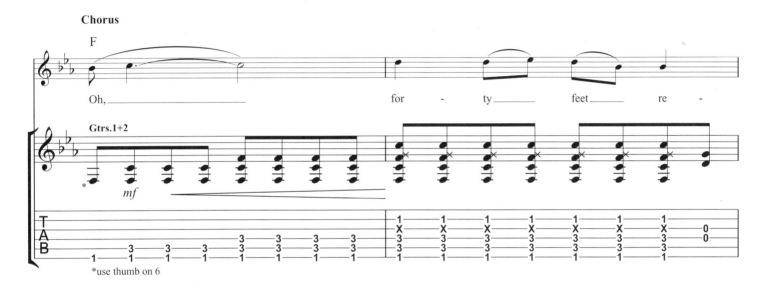

Oh, for - ty feet re -

*use thumb on 6

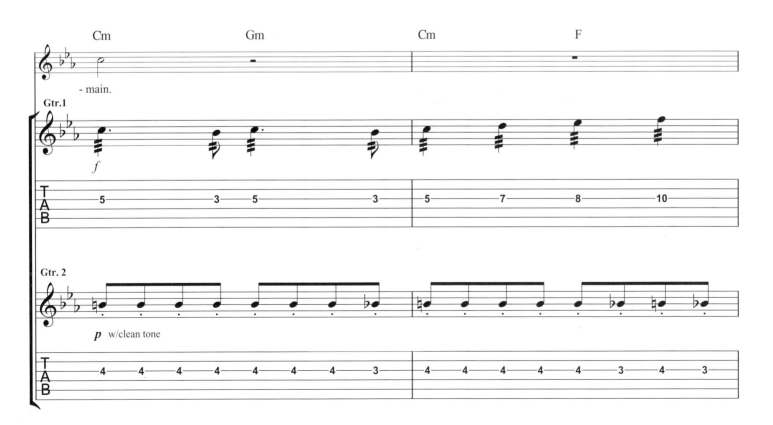

- main.

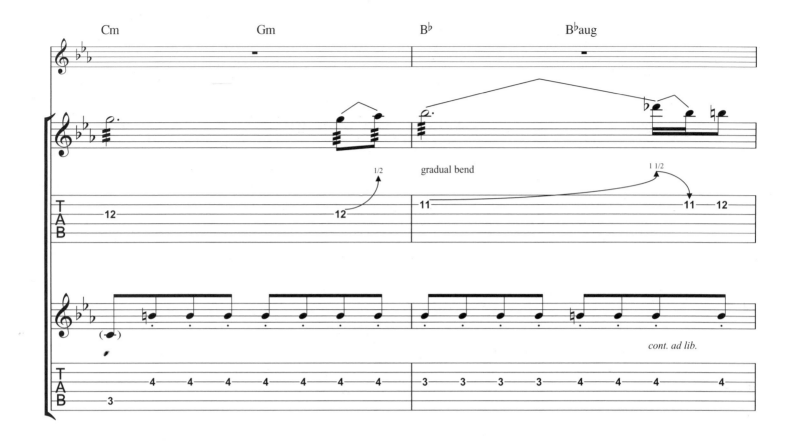

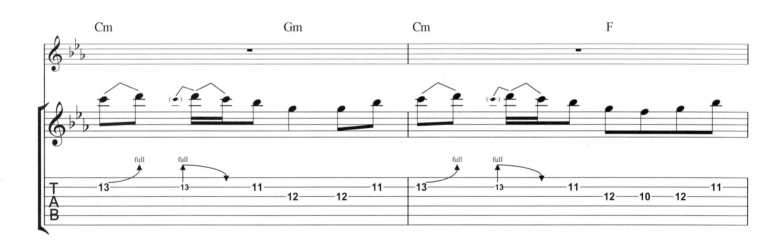

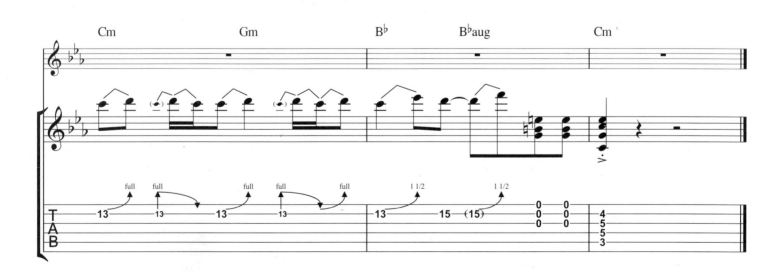

123456789